The B

R. E. Harlow

LUKE 24:27

Developed as a correspondence course by
Emmaus Correspondence School,
founded in 1942.

Published by:
ECS Ministries
P.O. Box 1028
Dubuque, IA 52004-1028
www.ecsministries.org

Cover Design
Ragont Design
Barrington, Illinois

ISBN 0-940293-33-1

Reprint 2006

Printed in United States of America

Instructions to Students

The Book of Acts tells us how the early church faced the challenge of the Great Commission. It tells how the gospel made its way westward until at last it settled at Rome. It is a book of people and places. It is also a book of principles, a book which sets before us a blueprint for world evangelism.

You will find this study of Acts basically simple yet stimulating and satisfying. It is not intended to be an in-depth study of the book. It is a fast-moving survey of those stirring events which changed all history for the rest of time. We trust it will be a challenge and a blessing to you.

Lessons You Will Study

1. The Book Itself
2. The Coming of Pentecost (1—2)
3. Triumph and Testing (3—5)
4. A Martyr and a Missionary (6—8)
5. Two Key Conversions (9—10)
6. Growing Pains (11—12)
7. The Regions Beyond (13—15)
8. The Second Round (16:1—18:22)
9. More Worlds to Conquer (18:23—20:38)
10. Paul Is Arrested (21—24)
11. The Appeal to Caesar (25—26)
12. Perils and Prison (27—28)

Course Components

This course has two parts: this textbook and the exam booklet.

The Study Course

The study course contains the lesson material you will use in your studies.

The Exam Booklet

The exam booklet contains all the exams for this course.

How to Study

Begin by asking God to open your heart to receive the truths He would teach you from His Word. Read each chapter through at least twice, once to get the general idea of its contents and then again, slowly, looking up all Scripture references and examining all footnotes. Remember, you may use a dictionary for any terms you do not understand. Do remember to read the relevant chapters from the Bible.

Exams

All the exams are in the Exam Booklet. Before taking each exam, carefully review the relevant chapter material including the Bible references. When you actually come to take the exams, try to do so without reference to the chapter, your Bible or your notebook unless otherwise instructed. The Exam Booklet contains more instructions.

Study Schedule

Begin studying immediately, or if you are in a group, as soon as the group begins. We suggest that you try to complete one chapter each week and take a maximum of one year to finish the course.

What Do You Say? Questions

You may freely state your own opinions in answer to such questions. Your candid answers will help your instructor to get to know you better as an individual. They will also help us evaluate the general effectiveness of this course.

How Your Papers Are Graded

Any incorrectly answered questions will be marked by your instructor. You will be referred back to the place in the Bible or the textbook where the correct answer is to be found. You will receive a certificate showing your grade.

Returning Your Exams

See the Exam Booklet for more information on returning your exams.

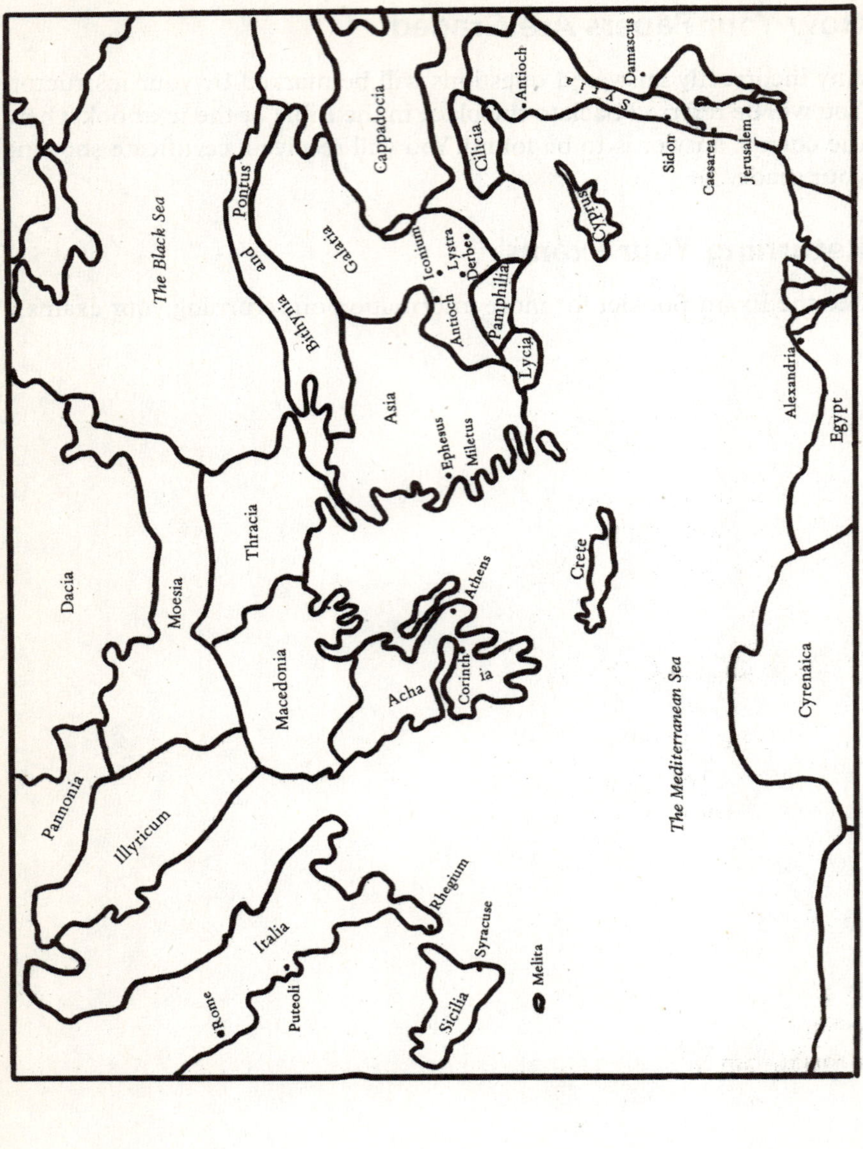
The Black Sea
Pontus
and
Bithynia
Galatia
Cappadocia
Cilicia
Antioch
Damascus
Syria
Sidon
Caesarea
Jerusalem
Cyprus
Iconium
Lystra
Derbe
Antioch
Pamphilia
Lycia
Asia
Ephesus
Miletus
Alexandria
Egypt
Dacia
Moesia
Thracia
Macedonia
Athens
Crete
Acha
ia
Corinth
The Mediterranean Sea
Cyrenaica
Pannonia
Illyricum
Italia
Rhegium
Syracuse
Melita
Sicilia
Puteoli
Rome

CHAPTER

1

The Book Itself

Memory Verses

Acts 1:8; 2 Timothy 3:16-17

Main Points of the Lesson

1. The whole Bible is the Word of God and every part of the Bible is important.
2. Acts tells us the work of the Holy Spirit.
3. Christ is alive and able to help us every day.

The New Testament

There are 27 books in the New Testament written by eight different people. Five of these tell the story of the Lord Jesus (the Gospels) or of the early church (Acts). Twenty-one are letters or epistles written to churches or individual persons. The last is the book of Revelation which tells of things to come.

Acts is a very important book because it tells how the Church started and grew. In the Gospels we read of the life and death of Christ (see Mark 1:1) and that, when He arose, He told His disciples to go everywhere and preach the gospel (see Matthew 28:18-20). The letters of Paul and others are written to churches in various parts of the world (see 1 Corinthians 1:1-2). Acts tells us how the disciples obeyed the Lord in spreading the gospel and how these churches were started.

The Acts

The most ancient name of this book is simply ACTS. Men have called it the Acts of the Apostles, but only Peter and Paul are prominent and the other apostles are mentioned only briefly. The real Person who is acting in and through the apostles is the Holy Spirit, who is referred to about seventy times in the book. Acts of the Holy Spirit would be a good name for this book.

Christ promised that the Father would send the Holy Spirit (1:8) and this promise was fulfilled a few days later (2:4). Peter was filled with the Holy Spirit when he was called up before the high priests (4:8) and so was Stephen when the Jews were going to kill him (7:55). You can find many more verses like these telling of the Acts of the Holy Spirit.

Who Wrote the Book of Acts?

"All Scripture is given by inspiration of God" and "Holy men of God spake as they were moved by the Holy Ghost." These verses and hundreds of others show us that it was God who told different men what to put down when they wrote the Bible. Still it is interesting to learn what we can about the authors.

Luke was a doctor (Colossians 4:14) and travelled with Paul on some of his long journeys. When telling about these travels, Luke uses the word "we" to say what Paul and he did or where they went. In other parts of the book he naturally says "he" or "they" did this or that. (Read 16:10; 20:6; 27:1.) He was also with Paul at the end of his life, just before Paul was put to death for the sake of the gospel (2 Timothy 4:11).

Why Did Luke Write Acts?

Luke wrote the Gospel of Luke as if it were a letter to an important man called Theophilus. It told the story of what Jesus *began* to do and teach (see Acts 1:1). You might think that since the gospel story ends with the death of Christ, there would not be much more to tell. But Luke wrote this book to tell Theophilus the story of what Jesus *continued* to do and teach, after His death. For Jesus did not only die for our sins, He rose again and then went back to heaven. In heaven He continued to work with His disciples. See Mark 16:20, "the Lord working with them."

We speak of Christ's finished work on the cross. Never forget His glorious "unfinished" work today in heaven, praying for us, leading and guiding, and working with us. Luke in his second book wanted to tell about this part of Christ's work when He had gone back to heaven (Hebrews 7:25).

What Is Acts About?

We have noticed that the book of ACTS tells about the work of Jesus in and through His own who are still down here on earth. He told them in 1:8 that they would be His witnesses both in Jerusalem, and in all Judea, and in Samaria, and unto the uttermost part of the earth. This is one of the key verses in the whole book.

Now Jerusalem was the holy city of the Jews, located in the land of Judea. The next country to it was Samaria, although the Jewish people did not get along very well with the people of Samaria. So Christ told the disciples to witness for Him first right where they were, then in their home land. Then they must go to their near neighbors, even though they did not like them. But then they were to spread out all over the whole world and tell people about the Lord. See also Mark 16:15-16 and Luke 24:46-48. If you are saved, Christ expects you to witness for Him wherever you are, and to be ready to go to a distant land as a missionary, if He calls you.

Whom Does Acts Tell About?

While the main persons in Acts are Peter (chapters 1—12) and Paul (chapters 13—28), there are around 80 different people mentioned in the book. Some of these were very important, like John (3:1) who wrote five books in the New Testament; or Timothy (16:1-3), a young man who travelled around with Paul a good deal. Others are not well known but their names are given (for example 20:4). Each had a part to play in the great work of getting out the gospel. It is very important that each Christian know just what God would have him to do . . . then do it.

CHAPTER

2

The Coming of Pentecost (1—2)

Memory Verses

Acts 1:8; 2:24

Main Points of the Lesson

1. Many persons bore witness to the resurrection of Christ.
2. Christ went back to heaven, is now in glory, but He promised that He will return again.
3. He commanded us to witness for Him in the whole world.
4. God knows the hearts of all men.
5. The Holy Spirit is God's second great gift to men.
6. The Holy Spirit gives power to witness for Christ.
7. He also helps the Church to worship God.

The Lord Jesus Ascends to Heaven

1. Christ Arose (Acts 1:1-3)

Truly it is a wonderful thing that Jesus should rise from the dead. But since He is the Son of God, it would be quite unbelievable if anyone said that He remained in the grave. We can be sure that He did rise from the dead, because there were many witnesses who saw Him during forty days after He had risen and before He went back to heaven. Some of these men, for example, Matthew, John and Peter have written books which tell us about Jesus rising from the dead. God has kept these books during all these years, and now we have them in our Bibles. So we can be quite certain that Jesus died and also rose again.

But if He rose from the dead, it must show that God accepted His work on the cross. Therefore men did very badly when they put Him to death. A still greater sin is to reject Him as Savior. Have you really accepted Him as your own Savior and Lord?

2. Commands and Promises (1:4-8)

Before Christ went back to heaven, He commanded His disciples to remain in Jerusalem for a while. Perhaps they wanted to go back home and get to work with their fishing nets again. Or maybe they wanted to start right out and tell everybody about the Lord Jesus, how He had died for our sins and rose again. In fact He had already told them to go into all the world and preach the gospel to every creature. But the time for this had not yet come, and so He tells them to wait for a while.

It is very important to do just what Jesus says even though we cannot understand the reason. . . . Sometimes we even want to do something for the Lord in a hurry, before the right time comes. But we should do what He wishes, and just when He wants us to do it.

Then He promised them the most wonderful of all gifts. He said that although they could not know when the Kingdom of God would come to earth, yet they would receive in a few days' time the Holy Spirit of God to abide with them forever. The Holy Spirit would give them power to go everywhere and witness for Jesus.

The disciples obeyed the command of the Lord in verse 8. We see in chapters 1—7 of Acts that they witnessed in the city of Jerusalem. Then in chapters 8—12 they witnessed for the Lord in the land of Judea and Samaria. After that, chapters 13—28, they preached everywhere, especially the apostle Paul and those who went with him.

3. Jesus Ascends to Heaven (1:9-11)

In John 1:14 we read that the Word (another name for the Son of God) became flesh and dwelt among men. In John 16:28 He said that He had come forth from the Father into the world and would soon go back to the Father. Here in today's lesson we see Him going back to heaven, to His Father. This should make us very glad, because Jesus loves His Father and we know that the Father loves His Son. He came a long journey into this world to do His Father's will. What a joy is theirs now that they are together again in heaven!

The disciples were so surprised that they stood there gazing up into heaven. So two angels appeared to them and told them plainly that this very same Jesus would come back again in the same way as He had gone into heaven. Those of us who love Him will be very glad to see Him when He comes. But if you are not yet saved, your last chance will be gone when Jesus comes back again. Why not accept Him now as your own Savior?

4. The Disciples Return to Jerusalem (1:12-14)

Jesus ascended to heaven from the Mount of Olives, near Bethany. After the angels told the disciples that He would surely come again, they returned to Jerusalem, about two miles away. They stayed there, as the Lord had commanded, and spent the days in prayer in an upper room. Prayer is a wonderful privilege and every true Christian should seek the Lord's face in prayer every day.

Who were these disciples? There are eleven names given, and we see that they were the same as those the Lord had first called, in Luke 6: 13-16. But one of the first twelve is no longer with them. He loved money rather than the Lord, listened to the voice of Satan, and sold Jesus for thirty pieces of silver. When Judas realized what he had done, he went out and killed himself.

Others who were praying in the upper room were the faithful women who had followed and loved the Lord. One of them was Mary the mother of the Lord, and with her were his brothers. These brothers did not believe on Christ at first (John 7:5) but after His death and resurrection, they realized that He was truly the Son of God, the Savior of the world.

5. Choosing a Substitute for Judas (1:15-22)

Peter realized that some one should be appointed to take the place of Judas, who had fallen into sin, and committed suicide. He remembered a verse in the book of Psalms which says that another should take his place. It is a terrible thing to have a work to do for God, but through sin, to have another take it over. But God cannot use in His service one who lives in sin.

So they selected two men who had also been with the Lord Jesus from the beginning and were witnesses of His death and resurrection. Their names were Joseph and Matthias.

6. *Prayer and Casting Lots Indicate Matthias (1:23-26)*

The apostles prayed to the God who knows the hearts of all men, then they cast lots to see which of the two was God's choice. The lot fell on Matthias, who was therefore numbered with the apostles, although we never hear of him again. Now that the Holy Spirit has been given we do not need to cast lots to know God's mind. But we can know His will by praying. And remember, He who knows our hearts knows our sins too. He is ready to forgive them if we ask in the name of Jesus.

The Coming of the Holy Spirit

1. *Signs: Wind, Fire, Tongues (2:1-4)*

The day of Pentecost was one of the feast days of the ancient Jews. It was held 50 days after the feast of Firstfruits (Leviticus 23:16). The feast of Firstfruits was held soon after the Passover, the day on which the Lord Jesus died. In 1:3 we saw that Jesus was with His disciples for forty days after His resurrection. So, soon after Christ went back to heaven, the Holy Spirit came to earth.

The 120 disciples were all together in one place when they heard the sound of wind, saw tongues of fire, and began to speak in other languages which they did not know before. How could God's Holy Spirit come and dwell with men whose hearts had been stained with sin? It would only be possible if those hearts had first been cleansed. What is sufficient to wash away the guilt of sin? The coming of the Holy Spirit shows how completely the blood of Christ washes away all our sin. And if He dwells in your heart, He will be grieved if any sin is permitted to dwell there too.

2. *Witnessing in Many Languages (2:5-11)*

Jewish people had been scattered all over the world, but some of them came back to Jerusalem, their holy city. Especially at the time of the feast many pilgrims would come to worship. Imagine the surprise of these people when they heard the disciples speaking in fifteen different languages!

What were they speaking about? "The wonderful works of God" (v. 11). In John 16:13-14 we read that the Holy Spirit would not speak of Himself, but would glorify Christ. So when a Christian is filled with the Holy Spirit, he will not talk about himself nor even about the Spirit, but about Christ and the wonderful works of God.

But some people did not understand and could only think that the disciples must be drunk with new wine. So today, even when we speak about Christ, many people will laugh and think we are very foolish. The important thing is to please God and not worry about what people say or think.

3. Peter Denies That They Had Been Drinking (2:12-15)

When some of the people insult the disciples by saying they must be drunk, Peter does not become angry, but quietly replies this is not the case at all. For one thing, people who drink wine do so at night, not early in the morning, and are not usually drunk at 9 o'clock. Besides, during the days of the Feast, they did not either eat or drink until after 9 o'clock, which was time for prayer. If my body is the dwelling place of the Holy Spirit, I should not eat or drink anything which is harmful to the body.

4. The Promise of Joel: The Spirit to Be Given (2:16-24)

After denying that the disciples were full of wine, Peter goes on to show that they are full of the Holy Spirit. In fact, he told them of a promise God gave long before to Israel through the prophet Joel that God would pour out His Spirit on all the people. This promise is found in the book of Joel 2:28-32. On the day of Pentecost, only some of the people received the Holy Spirit, but the time is coming when some from all nations will receive Him, when the Lord comes back again.

The last part of Joel's promise was true in Peter's day and is true today: "Whosoever shall call on the name of the Lord shall be saved." This means to believe in Christ and ask Him to forgive your sins. If you do, you will be saved. Although this promise is true today, it will not be true forever, and may not be much longer. If you are not sure you are saved, trust Him now.

And so Peter went on to preach about Christ. Although God had approved the work of Christ, wicked men took Him and nailed Him to a tree. God knew in advance that this would happen and soon brought His Son back to life again. In fact it was impossible that the Son of God should be kept in the place of death. Still the people were completely guilty of the murder of Christ and must repent and confess it before God could forgive.

5. The Promise of David: Christ Would Arise (2:25-36)

Peter went on to prove that even in the Old Testament, God had told David His servant that the Christ would rise from the dead. David could not have been speaking about himself, as his grave was right there in Jerusalem. But he was a prophet (v. 30) and was speaking about Christ. There are a great many wonderful things about Christ in the Old Testament.

Not only did David tell about the resurrection of Christ, he also said that Christ would be glorified at God's right hand (v. 34). And so Peter shows the people their terrible sin in opposing God, because they killed the very One whom God had approved before and now had glorified. If you reject Christ, you are rejecting God too, and you will be in the same position as the Jews who crucified Him.

6. Those Who Received the Word Continued (2:37-47)

Some of those who heard Peter wanted at once to do something about it. So he told them to repent, and to show their true repentance by being publicly baptized. About 3000 did so that very day of Pentecost. What a joy that was to Peter, to all the disciples, to those who were just saved, and to the Lord Himself in heaven!

More than that, they continued (v. 42) in the apostles' doctrine and fellowship, and in breaking of bread, and in prayers. They also showed their true love to the other believers, by helping those who were poor. It is not enough merely to say that I am saved, nor even to be baptized. I must prove my faith by doing what is right every day. Only then will I know the full joy of being truly saved.

CHAPTER

3

Triumph and Testing (3—5)

Memory Verses
Acts 4:12; 5:29

Main Points of the Lesson

1. Salvation is in Christ only, even for the worst of sinners.
2. We should pray for God's glory and trust Him to answer.
3. We need boldness to tell others of Christ.
4. God cannot tolerate lying (Revelation 21:8).
5. When sin is put out blessing comes in.
6. It is foolish to try to resist God.

The Lame Man Is Healed

1. Peter and John Perform a Miracle (3:1-10)

As Peter and John went one day into the temple at three o'clock in the afternoon, some people were just bringing in a beggar. This man had been born lame, and was now over forty years old. Seeing Peter and John, he immediately asked them for a little help (vv. 1-3).

Peter did not have much money, and none for this purpose, but he did know the power of God, and so was able to give something far better that afternoon than all the rich people who entered the temple. In the name of Jesus, he took hold of the lame man's hand and raised him up. Immediately he received strength and began to walk and leap. He realized that to know the Lord Jesus is far better than to have all the money in the world.

This man asked for a little money but he got what was far better. When we ask God for a certain thing, He may give us something instead which will do us more good than what we wanted. We must trust His wisdom, love and power whenever we pray.

2. Peter Teaches the Onlookers (3:11-26)

This great miracle soon attracted the attention of a large number of people, who thought that Peter must be a very holy man to be able to do such a thing. So Peter told them that it was really through the power of Jesus of Nazareth that the man was healed. Then Peter went on to tell them about Jesus and warn them that they should repent of their sins. He said that Christ had entered into glory (v. 13) and was coming back again (vv. 19-21). He reminded them that Moses in the Old Testament had said long ago that this would be so.

Notice that Peter does not seek his own glory, but turns the thoughts of the people to Christ. When speaking to our friends, we may talk about various things for a while, but should seek an opening or opportunity to bring in the things of the Lord. To do this properly, it is necessary to know a good deal about Christ, and this will be found in the Bible.

3. Peter and John Are Arrested (4:1-12)

You might think it strange that they should be arrested for healing a lame man and preaching about Jesus. But the high priests and the Sadducees did not believe all the Bible, and they were the ones who had wanted Jesus to be crucified. Thus by praising the Lord Jesus, Peter was really blaming them for their terrible crime. We always find that religious people are the ones who hate the gospel of Christ the most and persecute those who are witnessing for Him.

When they are accused before the court, Peter admits that they did this good deed in the name of Jesus, then at once accuses the *judges* of killing the Christ (v. 10). His is the only name whereby we can be saved. And despite their terrible sin, if they accept Jesus, God will forgive them. Wonderful grace of God!

4. *Peter and John Are Released (4:13-22)*

Even the priests were surprised at the courage of Peter and John since they supposed that they were ignorant and unlearned men. It is true that they were fishermen but they had been taught by Jesus for three years, and were wiser by far than the high priests. Even their judges knew that they had been with Jesus (v. 13). Can people tell by your courage and testimony that you have been in the presence of Jesus?

They admitted also that a great miracle had been done (v. 16). But still they are unwilling to admit that they themselves had been wrong, so they threatened the disciples and commanded that they should not speak any more in the name of the Lord Jesus. How foolish of men to try and resist God!

But Peter and John declare that it is right to obey God rather than man (v. 19). Christians are commanded in the Bible to obey their parents and the laws of the land. But if parents or authorities try to keep you from obeying God's Word, it is necessary to *disobey* them, and do what will please God. So Peter and John say they cannot stop telling the things which they have seen and heard (v. 20).

5. *The Christians Pray (4:23-31)*

So they let them go, and as soon as they were free, they went to meet with other Christians, and they all had a time of prayer together. When you can do whatever you want, do you *choose* to be with Christians, or do you find it boring to pray and sing hymns? Only those who are born again really enjoy the presence of the Lord.

But note that the disciples did not pray that they would be delivered from being persecuted by the Jews. Rather they prayed that they might continue to witness boldly (v. 29) and that God would do great things to glorify His Son. Today we see the Lord doing great things in saving souls, and this is really much more important and more glorifying to Jesus than the healing of the lame and blind.

6. *The Christians Receive Power (4:32-37)*

When they prayed the house was shaken and they were filled with the Holy Spirit, and witnessed (as they had prayed they might) with great courage (v. 31). But they showed their love to God in another way also . . . by sharing with each other the things which they had (v. 32). Some even sold their land and gave the money to the apostles so that all could spend their time in serving the Lord. Barnabas was one of these, and we shall hear a great deal about him a little later on.

Now today Christians should work and help with their money the servants of the Lord who spend all their time in His work. In this way they will share in the reward which He will give when He comes.

Opposition from Satan

1. Ananias and Sapphira Tell a Lie (5:1-11)

We have already seen how Satan tried to hinder the work of the Lord by leading the priests and Sadducees to throw Peter and John into jail. In this chapter we see him causing trouble *within* the church by tempting two people to lie. Then he attacks the church from outside, and we see the priests putting the apostles in prison again.

At the end of chapter 4 we saw how the believers helped one another, even selling their lands so that others could continue preaching the gospel. They did this because they loved the Lord, not to be honored by men. But two of them wanted to get this honor from men, without really giving all to God. So Ananias and Sapphira agreed to *say* that the money they brought was the full price of the land.

But Peter considered (and rightly so) that this was lying not so much to men but to the Holy Spirit. As soon as they heard this they both dropped down dead and were taken out to be buried. We see from this that it is a terrible thing to lie at all, especially when the things of God are concerned. God can keep us from this sin.

2. Miracles of the Apostles (5:12-16)

No doubt death seems to be terrible punishment for telling a lie. But God is very desirous that His church should be kept clean and free from sin. Without this there can be no blessing. Remember the story of Achan in Joshua 7:25.

After sin in the church has been judged, there is always a time of blessing. So here in Acts 5 we read that the apostles were given special powers from the Lord to heal the sick of every kind. It was important in the beginning that the Jews should know for sure that the teaching of the apostles was really of God, and so He gave them these wonderful miracles. Now we have a different kind of miracle, and still more wonderful. The miracle of a changed life, a man used to sin now living for God, the Holy Spirit keeping us in our daily lives—these things should be sufficient to convince anyone that Christianity is true.

3. An Angel Delivers the Apostles from Prison (5:17-21)

But Satan soon gets busy again, and we find the apostles as a group this time (not merely Peter and John) in the common prison. But the angel of the Lord came by night and opened the prison door, and told them to keep on preaching the gospel in the temple. So early in the morning back they go and tell the people "all the words of this life." The gospel is a message of life. Those without Christ are dead in trespasses and in sins (Ephesians 2:1). When we tell them how to be saved we are showing them the way out of death and into life. We should also tell them not merely how to be saved, but "all the words" of this life. Christ told His disciples to teach "all things whatsoever I have commanded you."

4. Their Trial (5:21-28)

Meanwhile the high priest met with the whole council and sent officers to bring in the prisoners. Imagine their surprise when they found the doors still locked, the guards still standing outside, but no one within! Then someone else came and reported that they were preaching again in the temple. So the officers went and called them quietly asking them to come to the council meeting. The apostles were not afraid, because they knew that God could deliver them again, so they went with them.

You would think that the priests, when they knew that God had delivered them from prison, and given other miracles as well, would not want to resist God any longer. But instead of admitting that they were wrong before, they now accuse the apostles of disobeying their commands and trying to bring the blame of Jesus' death on them. We can see that miracles will help those with an open mind, but those blinded by Satan will not believe even though they see many miracles.

5. Peter's Speech: They Must Not Disobey God (5:29-33)

It was quite true that Peter blamed the chief priests and the Jews for crucifying the Lord Jesus, and he was not afraid to say so, even though he knew that it might cost him his life. But the marvelous thing is that despite this terrible crime God was still willing to offer forgiveness to all. In fact, only because of Christ's death could God possibly forgive the sins of anyone. Thus man is responsible for slaying the Son of God, but God has used that very sin to make salvation available to every man.

But unfortunately these men added yet more sin to their guilty hearts by trying to kill the apostles (v. 33). First they crucified the Lord Jesus, then they rejected God's offer of forgiveness through the Holy Spirit, then they attempted to kill the messengers of God! How shall they escape the judgment of hell? But the same question can be asked of all who go on in their sins. One thing always leads to another, until finally the sinner's last chance of salvation is gone. If you have never really accepted the Lord Jesus as your own Savior, you had better do it now.

6. The Speech of Gamaliel: They Must Not Resist God (5:34-42)

First God had delivered His servants by an angel (v. 19). Now He uses one of the men in the council to speak on behalf of the apostles. Gamaliel was a wise man who helped in the education of the apostle Paul (22:3). But he never became a Christian, and what he says here was simply human wisdom. His point is that if this movement is merely of men, it will soon come to nothing. This is what happened to two men, Theudas and Judas, who gathered a lot of people by pretending that they were important persons. But they both died and their followers were soon scattered. On the other hand, if this movement were really of God, they should be careful lest they should be found actually to oppose God Himself! This advice helped the apostles, but of course, it does not mean that Gamaliel really believed on Jesus himself. He tried to remain neutral. But unless you come over from Satan's side to God's side, you will never be saved. You cannot remain on the fence.

So the apostles were released, and they went away rejoicing because they were able to suffer for the Lord Jesus who had done so much for them. Far from obeying the high priest, they continued to preach and teach the Lord Jesus, both publicly and in the homes of the people. May the Lord make us ready to suffer for Christ and serve Him every day!

CHAPTER

4

A Martyr and a Missionary (6—8)

Memory Verses
Acts 7:56; 8:22

Main Points of the Lesson

1. A Christian must be careful in money matters.
2. Satan uses various methods in attacking the church.
3. We should be ready to live or die for Christ.
4. Persecution of the church may be a good thing.
5. It is impossible to buy the gift of God.
6. We must obey God even when we can't understand.

The Work, Speech, and Death of Stephen

1. Seven Deacons Are Chosen (6:1-15)

The next trouble for the young church came when there was a complaint from some of the Grecians. These believers spoke Greek and were probably Jews. They felt that the Hebrew-speaking believers were not distributing the money fairly, so that widows of men in their group were being neglected. There is always a danger of people from different countries getting into a disagreement of some kind. But in Christ we are all one, and that is what counts the most.

The twelve apostles did not think it was right for them to stop preaching just to look after the money matters of the church, so they proposed that seven men should be appointed for this task. It is very important that money matters should be properly taken care of, both of the individual Christian and of the church.

The next form of trouble was again from outside the church, and some of the visitors to Jerusalem began to argue with Stephen about his doctrine. When they could not win the argument, they began to accuse him of speaking against the temple. Arguing seldom accomplishes anything useful.

2. Abraham Responded to the Promise of God (7:1-8)

When they brought Stephen to the council to accuse him, he thought it was a fine opportunity to show them the guilt of the Jewish people from the very beginning. So he started with the story of Abraham, who was the father of all the Israelites.

The full story of Abraham is given in Genesis 12—25. Here Stephen reminds them that God gave promises to Abraham, who believed and obeyed. Now these Jews who claim to be the sons of Abraham are unwilling to accept God's promises about Jesus, and are intent on killing His messenger! Those who know the truth and refuse it are capable of doing far worse things than those who never heard.

3. Joseph Is Envied Then Glorified (7:9-16)

Then Stephen goes on to the story of Joseph, who was the great grandson of Abraham. His ten brothers heard that he would be ruler over them and this made them jealous. God had chosen Joseph to be the chief of the sons of Jacob, so by rejecting Joseph, they were refusing God's will. The story of Joseph is in Genesis 39—50.

The Israelites were the sons of Joseph and his brothers, and Stephen here is saying that they too are rejecting the Man of God's choice, the Lord Jesus Christ. Joseph's brothers sold him as a slave for twenty pieces of silver, but God made him ruler over all the land. Christ had been sold for thirty pieces of silver, and God has now highly exalted Him.

4. Moses, Rejected at First, Became the Leader of Israel (7:17-43)

Now Stephen goes on to tell the story of Moses, who the Jews regarded very highly as the great Law-giver. Moses was educated as the son of Pharaoh's daughter, but he knew that God wanted him to deliver the people of Israel. So one day he saw an Egyptian fighting with one of the Israelites, and went to the help of his brother. The next day he tried to help two Israelites who were quarrelling, but they refused his help, and asked, "Who made you our Judge?"

But forty years later, God sent Moses back to Egypt to deliver Israel from the bondage of Pharaoh (v. 34) and now the people gladly receive him. Once again we see the people refused the man of God's choice, only to accept him later.

Stephen then reminds them of the very words of Moses himself (v. 37) spoken long before, promising the people of Israel that God would sometime raise up another prophet like himself. This was fulfilled when Jesus came (John 1:17) but they were still resisting Him. Even in the wilderness journey from Egypt to Canaan, when God was leading the people with a pillar of fire, they turned from Him and worshipped idols. The heart of man is always the same. Men have always rejected God, and refused the blessing He wants to give. Are you one of those who have accepted Christ and the blessing He offers?

5. From the Beginning the Jews Refused the Will of God (7:44-53)

The Jews had accused Stephen of saying that their wonderful temple would be destroyed (6:14). But he shows now that even the temple was not really according to God's will. Then he plainly declares (v. 51) that they have always resisted God's Holy Spirit. Their fathers had killed the prophets whom God had sent, and now they have killed the Son of God, the Lord Jesus Christ. Even the law which they received from God through angels they had not kept.

We must admire Stephen's bravery in so speaking before these men. He knew that they had power to kill him, if God permitted it. But he hoped some of them anyway would realize their terrible guilt, and cry to God for forgiveness. This is necessary, as people who do not realize that they are sinners, nor think that their sin is really so bad after all, do not feel any great need of a Savior. But when they see that God hates sin and will punish it forever, they are really glad to accept Christ as their own.

6. Stephen Falls Asleep (7:54-60)

Far from accepting this, however, the Jews become so mad that they gnash on him with their teeth. Then God gave Stephen a vision of heaven and there was Jesus standing at the right hand of God. When the people heard this, they let out a great cry, dragged poor Stephen out of the city, and threw huge stones at him until he died. But before he died, Stephen, as the Lord Jesus had done (Luke 23:34) prayed that God would forgive them.

Falling asleep for a believer is another way of saying that he died. Stephen was the first one to die for Jesus, but since then many thousands have done so. Are you ready to die for Him if necessary? If so, you will be willing to live for Him every day.

The Gospel Travels to Samaria and Africa

1. The Persecution of Saul and the Miracles of Philip (8:1-8)

We are particularly interested in Saul, whose name was mentioned for the first time when he helped in killing Stephen. We shall see later how he was converted to God and his name changed to Paul. At this time Saul was a rabbi or teacher of the Jews, like Nicodemus (John 3). But Saul was sure that this new teaching was of the devil and he did his best to stamp it out. Saul was born in Tarsus, a city of Cilicia, and was probably one of those who argued with Stephen in 6:9.

Having killed Stephen, the Jewish people thought that this was a good time to scatter and destroy all who believed in this man Jesus. As many as they could find they threw into prison, and the others, except the apostles themselves, fled to other countries.

But this only resulted in the spreading of the gospel still further, BECAUSE EVERYWHERE THE CHRISTIANS WENT THEY TOLD PEOPLE ABOUT THE LORD JESUS! Maybe persecution was necessary to make them obey the Lord's command. Anyway it resulted in blessing for many who heard and got saved.

One of the deacons chosen in chapter 6 to look after the money of the church (Stephen) was killed. Another, Philip, is now seen going to the city of Samaria and preaching there. Again the Lord gave special miracles and many of the Samaritans believed. The result was great joy in that city (v. 8).

2. Simon Believes and the Samaritans Receive the Spirit (8:9-17)

One of these Samaritans was a sorcerer named Simon who used to deceive the people by the power of Satan. Now he too hears the Word and believes and is baptized.

In John 4:9 we read that the Jews had no dealings with the Samaritans. But Christ had told the apostles to witness to Him not only in their own land (Judea) but also in Samaria (1:8). So now hearing of the blessing in the land of their ancient enemies, the apostles go down to Samaria, and when they had prayed, God showed that He had accepted them also by giving them the gift of the Holy Spirit. If we really love God, we will love men too, and never refuse to give them the gospel because we do not like them.

3. Simon Wants to Buy the Gift of God (8:18-25)

It seems a wonderful thing to Simon that the apostles could give the Holy Spirit merely by laying their hands on people. The money he had was probably received from the people by his former Satanic power. Now he wishes to use this to buy the special privileges of the apostles for himself. Peter tells him that unless he repents his money will perish with him. So Simon asks Peter to pray for him too.

To offer money for the gift of God was a terrible thing for Simon to do. Yet there are very many people today who think that by giving money to the church they will somehow win God's favor. But eternal life is a GIFT from God, and it is an insult to a person to offer to pay for a gift. God wants us to accept the Savior He has provided, then when we have become children of God, we can bring our gifts to Him to show our love for all He has done for us.

4. Philip Meets with the Eunuch from Ethiopia (8:26-29)

Now while all this blessing and joy is being seen in Samaria, Philip is suddenly called away to go to a desert place. It is very important that we should obey the commands of God even when we do not understand. When Philip got there, he met a great man from Ethiopia, a large country in Africa. This man had been to Jerusalem to worship God and was returning in his chariot to his own country.

In Jerusalem he had no doubt heard about Jesus, but he did not really understand or get peace. As he rides along, he is reading his Bible, which at that time consisted only of the Old Testament, as the New had not yet been written. So the Spirit said to Philip to go up and join the Ethiopian in his chariot.

Here we find a man who is seeking for the truth. He had been to Jerusalem, which was supposed to be the Holy City. But the Jews had very successfully driven away the Christians, who were the only ones who really knew the truth. So this man who came so far was returning unsatisfied. But God had a faithful servant (Philip) who obeyed His command and brought the light to this man. Let us be ready to obey at all times.

5. Philip Explains the Meaning of the Prophecy (8:30-35)

Now the Ethiopian had been reading in the book of Isaiah, which tells more about Christ than almost any book in the Old Testament. The 53rd chapter tells about the sufferings of Christ, but the Ethiopian was not sure whether the prophet was speaking about himself or someone else. So Philip began to explain to him that the prophet was really speaking about Christ, who had to suffer for our sins before He entered into His glory. If He had not suffered and died, He could have returned to the glory, because there was no sin on Him. But He would have remained alone in heaven forever, as no sin can enter heaven, and all men are sinners. The sad part is that even though He went through the awful agony of the cross, many even today still refuse to accept His salvation. Has His death been in vain as far as you are concerned?

6. Philip Baptizes the Ethiopian and Returns (8:36-40)

The Ethiopian immediately believed the grand story of the Lord Jesus, and to show his faith, asked if he could be baptized at once. This Philip was glad to do, but when he had finished, the Spirit took him away, and the Ethiopian saw him again no more. Nevertheless he had found Christ, and went on his way rejoicing. We can be sure that when he arrived back home he would lose no time in telling the Queen and all others about the suffering and glorified Savior. Thus the gospel got to Africa through the faithful obedience of one man, Philip.

So we see in chapter 8, the apostles are spreading out with the gospel, in obedience to the Lord's command. We who believe must be ready to serve Him wherever He sends us.

CHAPTER

5

Two Key Conversions (9—10)

Memory Verses
Acts 9:16; 10:35

Main Points of the Lesson

1. Christ is one with all His people.
2. Christians must be ready for persecution.
3. Bible stories about miracles are perfectly true.
4. Many people all over the world love God.
5. It is a sin to bow down before any person, dead or alive, except God.
6. We should love all who love the Lord Jesus.

Saul Believes in Christ

1. Saul Sees the Light (9:1-9)

Saul in his blind zeal for God and in his desire to become a great man among the Jews, now sought to persecute these Christians wherever they might be. So he went to the high priest and asked him for permission to go to Damascus and arrest all who believed in Christ whether men or women, and bring them back to Jerusalem. He was doing the work of Satan while thinking he was doing the work of God.

But when he got near Damascus, a strong light shone around them brighter than the brilliant noon sun. Then he saw the Lord Jesus, who asked him why he was persecuting Him. Saul might have said, "I am only persecuting the Christians"; but by attacking the Lord's people, he was attacking the Lord too. Christ is the Head of the Body, which is His Church, as Paul wrote long afterwards (Ephesians 1:22-23). The great surprise to Saul was that Jesus is indeed the Lord, and seated in the glory of heaven.

Jesus told him to go into the city and he would then be told what he should do. Now Saul was blinded by the light, but the men who were with him led him by the hand into Damascus.

2. Saul Is Baptized (9:10-19)

Then the Lord spoke to another faithful servant of His, whose name was Ananias. He told him to go to a certain house and lay his hands on Saul so that he might get his sight back again. At first Ananias was afraid, because he knew that Saul had come in order to arrest all Christians. So then the Lord showed him that Saul would become a great servant of Christ, and preach the gospel to many.

So Ananias went and laid his hands on Saul, calling him "Brother." Immediately he regained his sight and was baptized and filled with the Holy Spirit. We know nothing else about this man Ananias except what we read here. But he must have been walking with the Lord very closely to obey such a difficult command. And so Saul learned that the Lord is Head of the Church, and that He is able to speak to His servants and they will obey. He also learned that he was now "brother" to all those whom he had just so recently been persecuting. These are important lessons: that the church is all one and that each member must obey the commands of the Head.

3. Saul Preaches in Damascus (9:20-25)

Saul did not lose any time before he began to tell others about the Lord Jesus. This is a mistake some young believers make. At first they are afraid to tell their friends about Christ, then later on it becomes still harder to make a start. And every day you put it off it becomes still more difficult.

And for Saul it was more dangerous, because the Jews were very bitter against any who changed his religion. Saul himself had just been persecuting these Christians, and what could he expect from the Jews when he was converted?

Sure enough, after a while they made a plot to kill him and watched the gates of the city day and night in case he should try to escape. But the Christians let Saul down from the top of the wall in a basket, and so he got away. "All who will live godly in Christ Jesus shall suffer persecution."

4. Saul Preaches in Jerusalem (9:26-31)

Even after he had reached Jerusalem Saul's troubles were not over. At first the Christians were afraid to receive him, even as Ananias at first hesitated to obey the Lord's commands. But Barnabas, of whom we read in 4:36, came and helped Saul by telling the apostles his story. So they received him and once again he began to preach about the Lord Jesus.

Then we see the Greek Jews trying to kill him. When Stephen argued with them and showed them they were wrong, they brought him into the court and laid an accusation against him. But now these same people simply go about to slay Saul at once. Again the disciples help Saul to escape, and fifteen days after he had arrived (Galatians 1:18) he departed again, this time for Caesarea, and from there to Tarsus, his home city. After this the Lord gave a time of quiet and peace, and the churches grew and multiplied. But you can see how much it cost Saul to live the Christian life. We should be ready to live or die for Christ who gave His all for us.

5. Peter Heals Aeneas (9:32-35)

We shall soon come back to the story of Saul, later known as Paul, because the last half of Acts, from chapter 13 on, is mostly taken up with his activities. But now we hear some more of Peter's work, as the apostles fulfill the Lord's commands to witness in the land of Judea.

At Lydda, Peter found a man who had been sick for eight years. He told him that Jesus Christ would heal him, and immediately the man rose up and walked. This made such a tremendous impression on the people that all who dwelt in Lydda and the nearby town of Saron turned to the Lord. Some people today think that many of these old miracles were just imaginary, as if the man were not really sick at all. But here, for example, everybody knew that he had been sick for years, and when they saw the miracle which Peter had done, together they turned to the Lord. We can be sure that the Bible tells the truth, and means just what it says.

6. Peter Raises Dorcas (9:36-43)

Now Peter is given power to perform a still greater miracle, to raise Dorcas from the dead. Peter was still at Lydda when she died but the disciples sent for him to come to Joppa. He went alone into the room and prayed, then told her to arise. This miracle also convinced many that Peter was preaching the truth of God. But far more important even than raising a person from the dead is the fact that Peter gave them the gospel, and many got life eternal.

The House of Cornelius

1. Cornelius Sees a Vision of an Angel (10:1-8)

God had given wonderful promises to Abraham, Isaac and Jacob, and told them that He would especially bless their children. But when the Jewish people fell into sin, God had to punish them. At this time the Romans were ruling over the Jews, and in their troubles they prided themselves on these special promises which God had given to them as a nation. The result of this was that the Jews were unfriendly to other peoples, all of whom they called Gentiles.

Now Cornelius was a Gentile who feared God, helped poor people with various gifts, and prayed every day. And so God knew that he was ready to believe the gospel and sent an angel to show him the way. The angel told him to send to Joppa and ask Peter to come and tell him what he should do.

It is wonderful to know that God has many people in other countries who honor Him and try to do His will. He looks on the heart of all men and can tell those who have faith and really love Him. What does He see in your heart?

2. Peter Also Sees a Vision (10:9-16)

Cornelius immediately obeyed the word of the Lord and sent three men to ask Peter to come to him. The only way to get from Caesarea to Joppa was to walk and it was too far to go in one day. While they are on the way, Peter also sees a vision from heaven while he is waiting for his meal to be prepared.

In his vision Peter sees a great vessel with all sorts of animals on it. Now Jewish people were not allowed to eat most kinds of meat, just as they were not allowed to keep company with those who were not Jews. So when the voice from heaven tells him to kill one of the animals and eat some food, he refused to do so. But the voice told him that if God had cleansed anything, it was clean. And just to make sure that Peter would understand, this was done three times.

Peter was hungry for food, but we know that he was desirous to win souls for Christ too. So God showed him that there were many persons whom he thought to be unclean, but were really ready to hear the gospel of God's grace. It is the same today. We must be faithful in speaking to people about the Lord Jesus.

3. Peter Obeys the Holy Spirit (10:17-22)

At first Peter did not understand the meaning of this vision. But when the three men from Cornelius arrived, the Holy Spirit told him to go with them without any fear. Now the day before Peter would certainly have hesitated to be seen in the company of three Gentiles, but in the vision, God had told him not to call any man common or unclean. So he immediately introduced himself and asked them what they wanted. Then the next day with six other Christians he set out with them on the long walk to Caesarea.

It is a good thing for a Christian to be ready to obey God's voice, as heard in the Holy Scripture, no matter whether he understands at first or not. A little child cannot always know the reason for certain things that his father tells him to do or not to do. But later on he will understand and be grateful to a wise and loving father for guiding him.

4. Peter Arrives at the House of Cornelius (10:23-33)

Cornelius was sure that Peter would arrive and so he invited many friends to come and hear the message. So there they were all waiting for him as soon as he arrived. Now Cornelius loved God, but did not know the Bible very well. He felt that Peter must be some great man, so he fell down to worship him.

But this Peter immediately refused to accept, saying that he was only a man, not God. Actually it is a terrible sin to bow down before another man and worship him. Millions of people do that very thing today, worshipping some ancient person, or some living person. It is obvious that Peter would never do such a thing, nor did Cornelius as soon as he learned better. But he repeated the story again to Peter of how he had seen the angel, and had sent to Joppa to call him.

5. Peter Preaches Christ (10:34-43)

Now Peter really understands the meaning of the vision which he had seen. God does not favor one nation above another, but wherever He sees a man with faith in his heart, and a willingness to do the will of God, He can accept him and forgive his sins. The man may not even know the story of Christ and His death for sinners, but God does, and He can forgive sins for Christ's sake, if a man will accept it. But as Christians, our responsibility is to tell others about Christ, even if they do not want to hear, as they may learn to love Him if they hear about Him from us.

So Peter goes on to tell Cornelius and all that were there, the wonderful story of love, how Christ went about doing good but was killed by wicked men; yet God raised Him on the third day. Peter and the other apostles were witnesses of these things, and even in the Old Testament, the prophets of God had told that they would come to pass.

6. Cornelius Receives the Holy Spirit and Is Baptized (10:44-48)

But even before Peter had ended what he wanted to say, all those who heard believed the Word, accepted Christ as their own Savior, and the Holy Spirit came upon them. The six men who had come with Peter were indeed surprised to see that God's Holy Spirit came on the Gentiles just as He had upon them in the beginning. But they knew that this was of the Lord, so no one could refuse to baptize Cornelius and all that were with him. God could not possibly give the Holy Spirit to one whose heart was full of sin and corruption. We can see that they truly believed, their sins were washed away, and so they were baptized right away.

We must be prepared to receive all who truly love the Lord Jesus, even though they come from a different race than our own. Christ told all Christians to love one another, and this will be the sign that the world shall know we belong to Him.

CHAPTER

6

Growing Pains (11—12)

Memory Verses
1 John 3:14; Acts 12:24

Main Points of the Lesson

1. I should be very careful about criticizing others.
2. Possessing the Holy Spirit and loving other Christians are two signs that I am saved.
3. "Christians" is a good name for those who believe in Christ.
4. Those who follow the Lord Jesus are on the right side.
5. God helps those who pray and help themselves.
6. Though the wicked seem to prosper their judgment will come.

Jerusalem and Antioch

1. The Jewish Christians Criticize Peter (11:1-3)

In chapter 10 we saw that God gave Peter a special vision to teach him he must be willing to preach the gospel to Gentiles as well as Jews. It was thought to be a very bad thing for a Jew to go into the house of someone who belonged to another nation, and eat a meal with him.

So when Peter got back to Jerusalem, the Jewish Christians began to criticize him for what he had done. No doubt it was God's will that this narrow view should be set aside, but even Peter, who had been especially commanded by the Lord to teach all nations, required a direct revelation from God to make him cast aside his own feelings.

Even so, it is well to consider carefully before we begin to criticize anyone, especially another Christian or a servant of the Lord. The word "Devil" means "Accuser," and his work is to accuse the brethren (Revelation 12:10). On the other hand, Christ is called the Advocate (1 John 2:1) which means that He is always ready to defend His people from accusations. God alone knows all the circumstances, and the motives of the heart, so He alone can judge His servants.

2. Peter Explains Why He Went to Cornelius' House (11:4-14)

Sometimes when people begin to criticize us for our actions, especially some service for the Lord, we may get annoyed and resent their interference. Instead of that, Peter simply begins to explain how the Lord has led him in this matter from the beginning.

The Lord Jesus said that man must give account of every idle word which he speaks. We can be sure that the Holy Spirit in writing Scripture does not repeat anything without a good reason. Here in this chapter we have a repetition of what we read in the last. This is not a mere waste of time. We can understand by this repetition that it was a very important step when Peter finally became willing to preach to the Gentiles as well. What is *your* true reason for not wanting to tell others about Christ?

3. The Holy Spirit Is a Proof of Salvation (11:15-18)

The Lord Jesus had specially promised that the believers would receive the gift of the Holy Spirit. Could there be any greater sign and proof of the love of God, or of the cleansing power of the blood of Christ, than that God's Holy Spirit should come and dwell in our hearts (John 7:39)?

Peter's final argument is that God showed His acceptance of these Gentile believers by giving them the Spirit. Thus there was no difference between Jew and Gentile. Both must be saved by faith, both are indwelt by the same Spirit of God.

When they heard this, even the Jewish believers rejoiced to know that God's grace extended to the Gentiles. This is another sign that one is saved, that he really loves other believers in the Lord Jesus. (See 1 John 3:14; 5:2.) Do you KNOW that you have been born again?

4. At Antioch, the Disciples Preach to Jews and Greeks (11:19-21)

Before Saul was saved, he caused such a bitter persecution against the Christians that they all left Jerusalem except the apostles. This turned out to be a good thing, because everywhere they went they preached the gospel, but only to Jews. They had not yet learned the lesson of Peter, that God was equally ready to save Gentiles.

But some of those who got as far as Antioch had been born in Cyprus and Cyrene. They were not quite as narrow-minded as the Jews of Jerusalem, and felt free to speak to Greeks. These were delighted to hear how they could be saved, and a great number believed and turned to the Lord.

Looking back we can see a progress in the preaching of the gospel. Up to the time that Stephen was stoned, the disciples remained in the city of Jerusalem. Then we see Philip and the apostles at Samaria, and the eunuch takes the gospel back to Ethiopia. Then Saul after he was converted preached in Damascus, and Peter in Lydda and Joppa and to Gentiles in Caesarea. Now here in Antioch many Grecians are saved by faith. The student should look up these places on a Bible map.

5. Barnabas and Saul (11:22-26)

When the news of this blessing got back to Jerusalem, there was nothing but joy. Do you remember what happened when news of Samaria and Caesarea reached Jerusalem? This time the apostles sent forth Barnabas, of whom we have heard in chapters 4 and 9. He was very glad to see what the Lord had done, and exhorted the people to continue walking with the Lord.

Then he went off to Tarsus to look for Saul so that he too could come and help in the work. Saul was glad to do this, and so the two of them stayed a whole year teaching the people the Word of Christ. So much did they talk about Christ and seek to glorify Him that the people of that city began to call them Christians, which means "Christ's ones." This is a good name for us. Many Christians today have taken other names which show that they are not the same as all Christians. But it is well not to glory in any name except what the Bible calls us: saints, disciples, believers, Christians, brethren.

6. A Prophet Tells of the Coming Famine (11:27-30)

Then came some prophets from Jerusalem, including Agabus, who said that there would be a great famine. So the disciples decided to send some money to Jerusalem to help the poor saints there. They chose Saul and Barnabas to take this money to the elders of the church there. We saw before that love to the brethren was a sure sign of being born again. And these people had been helped spiritually by the saints at Jerusalem, so they wished to help them with material things.

Persecution at Jerusalem

1. James, the Brother of John, Is Killed (12:1-2)

There are three kings called Herod in the New Testament. The first is mentioned in Matthew 2. He was reigning when Jesus was born, and he tried to kill "Him that was born King of the Jews" because he wanted to be king himself. Another Herod was ruler of Galilee when Jesus was killed. He cut off the head of John the Baptist, and came to an agreement with Pilate about the Lord Jesus at the time of His death (Luke 23:12).

The king spoken of in our portion for today was grandson of the first, and shared with both of them a fierce hatred of everyone connected with the name of Christ. And so here we see him without any cause killing James with the sword.

There are also at least three men called James in the New Testament. This one and another were apostles and are mentioned by name in Matthew 10:2-3. Another, a brother of the Lord (Mark 6:3), wrote the epistle of James, and is referred to in verse 17 of this chapter too.

What a contrast between the Herods and the Jameses! From this verse you would think that Herod was stronger, but when Jesus comes and all is judged, it will be seen that those who, like James, have followed the Lord were really on the right side. Which side are you on?

2. Peter Put in Prison by Herod and Released by an Angel (12:3-10)

For the time, however, Herod thought that he was very successful, and so he proceeded to imprison Peter. He did it to please the Jews. How many have fallen into sin because they wished to please men! Just to make sure, he put Peter under the care of sixteen soldiers.

But the church was praying for Peter, and so God sent an angel to bring him out. Peter was so full of confidence and peace that even though he was to stand trial the next day, we find him sound asleep. The angel told him to get up and follow him. The chains fell off his hands, and the great prison doors opened of themselves. But when the angel brought Peter out into the street, he saw that now Peter could manage for himself, and so left him.

So we note here that no power on earth can resist the will of God, that God will do great things to help His own in answer to prayer, but that He expects us to do for ourselves what we can.

3. Peter Goes to His Brethren (12:11-17)

At first Peter could hardly realize what had taken place. But when he did, he knew that he was free again, and so he went to the place where other believers were. What do you do when you are free, no longer bound by work or school hours? Do you seek the company of those who are "of like precious faith," to enjoy fellowship with them?

Here it was the middle of the night, and these people were so in earnest that they were still praying to God for Peter. Yet when their prayer is answered so wonderfully by God, and Peter appears at the door, they cannot believe that God has really heard them. Actually their faith was not very strong, yet God honored it. But when we ask, we should really believe that God hears and will answer. Only thus can we truly glorify the Lord.

4. The Prison Guards Are Put to Death (12:18-19)

It was a very great crime for a guard to let his prisoner escape. It was assumed that the prisoner had given him a large gift to let him get away, and so in the Roman Empire, if a guard did not carefully keep his prisoner, he could be put to death. Actually Herod was himself afraid, as he had a good idea that these Christians really knew the power of God. He did not at all believe the guards' story, and ordered that they should be put to death.

When Jesus had been crucified, Joseph buried Him in a new tomb, which Pilate sealed lest the disciples should steal the body and say that He had risen from the dead. But of course not even the stone in front of the tomb, the whole Roman army, nor all the forces of Satan together could keep the Son of God in the grave. The guards were in danger of losing their lives too, but the priests promised to protect them if it was found out (Matthew 28:11-15). How foolish men are to resist God! He is sure to overcome in the end. Yet many reject Christ, and try to go on in a path of sin, knowing quite well that some day God will judge them.

5. Herod Is Judged (12:20-23)

Many people seem to get away with their sins for a long time, but here we see the judgment of God soon falling on this wicked man. Some of the people came to beg his favor, and he made a great speech. Those who heard were anxious to flatter the king, so they cried out that it must be the voice of a god and not of a mere man. Instead of giving God the glory, and admitting that he was only a man, Herod greatly enjoyed this false praise. The result was that an angel of God smote him with worms and he died a humiliating death.

We can be sure that all who resist God and reject Christ will some day meet their righteous judgment. But it is often very hard to understand when wicked people seem to prosper and nothing happens to them. However, when God's time comes, all will be plain.

6. Barnabas and Saul and Mark (12:24-25)

The persecution which killed James and put Peter into prison ended when God judged the wicked Herod. Despite Satan's efforts, the word of God grew and multiplied. Always after a time of trouble God brings us into a happy time of blessing.

Barnabas and Saul had come from Antioch to Jerusalem to bring some money for the Christians there (11:30). When they finished this work, back they went to Antioch, and with them the young man, John Mark. His family owned a large house where the Christians had met together for prayer (v. 12). He had been greatly impressed with these things and had a real desire to serve the Lord too. He was a cousin of Barnabas (Colossians 4:10) and so he went along with the apostles to Antioch.

CHAPTER

7

The Regions Beyond (13—15)

Memory Verses
Acts 13:39; 15:11

Main Points of the Lesson

1. The Old Testament teaches a great deal about Christ.
2. Most of the Jewish people rejected the gospel.
3. Persecution should not keep us from serving the Lord.
4. Good works cannot save anyone.
5. Good works cannot keep anyone saved.
6. Good works are essential to show my love to God for saving me.

Paul's First Missionary Journey

1. Paul and Barnabas Sent Forth (13:1-12)

In the church at Antioch, besides Saul and Barnabas, there were three other Bible teachers. As they waited on the Lord in prayer, the Holy Spirit told them to send forth these two for a special work which He had for them. No doubt Saul and Barnabas were ready for this call, and the other Christians in the church were happy to send them out in this way. Both the missionaries and the church were obedient to the leading of the Holy Spirit.

The first place they visited was the island of Cyprus, and John Mark went with them to help in the work. When they had gone through the whole island preaching the gospel, they came to a man in charge of the country, named Sergius Paulus. This man was interested in the Word but Elymas the sorcerer tried to keep him from the truth. Finally Paul (as he is called from this time onward) punished him with blindness for a while so that he would stop opposing the spread of the gospel light. Then Sergius Paulus believed in the Lord. . . . It is a terrible thing to resist the light of the truth. After a while, a person loses his ability to know what the truth is—he becomes blind—and will more easily believe a lie of Satan.

2. Paul's Speech at Antioch in Pisidia: Christ Died (13:13-29)

From Cyprus they returned to the mainland, into a rather dangerous district. At this point John Mark returns to Jerusalem. We do not know just why Mark turned back, but it is true that many young people start off bravely enough in the Lord's work, but soon drop out again. This is very sad, as the Lord loves a faithful servant.

Soon the other two arrive at another city called Antioch, in the land of Pisidia. Paul always went first to the synagogue and there found an opportunity to preach the gospel of Christ to the Jews. Here we have a record of his message, and no doubt in other places he often spoke along the same lines.

First he refers them to the Old Testament story, as Stephen had done before. Then as soon as possible he starts speaking about the Lord Jesus Christ (v. 23). He tells them of His forefathers, that He was in the line of King David; of His forerunner, John the Baptist; of His rejection by the Jews, the very ones to whom He had been sent; and of His death, which was itself a fulfillment of Old Testament prophecy. To speak well of Christ, one should know both the Old Testament and the New. Both tell something of the wonderful story of our Redeemer.

3. Paul's Message: Christ Rose Again from the Dead (13:30-41)

Of course it would not make the people happy to be told that Christ had died on the cross. And so Paul goes on at once to tell of His glorious resurrection from among the dead. There were many witnesses of this fact, and Paul also quotes from the Old Testament, from the book of Psalms to prove that this must be so. Then through this Man, Paul says, they may have the forgiveness of sins, and warns them of the results if they refuse God's offer. It is possible to think that Christ was a wonderful Man, without actually believing on Him for salvation. Those who do not believe cannot be saved.

4. The Results of Paul's Message in Antioch (13:42-52)

Jews, Gentiles who believed in God, and others as well, all wanted to hear Paul preach again the next Sabbath, so much so that almost the whole city came out to hear him. This was too much for the unbelieving Jews, who had never been able to get such a large crowd to hear them. They therefore began to argue with Paul and to contradict and blaspheme. So Paul and Barnabas said they would be forced to turn to the Gentiles as they had been commanded by the Lord. This, of course, made the Gentiles glad, but the Jews got more and more angry, until finally they stirred up so much trouble that the apostles had to leave the city. But they left behind them a company of happy disciples who were glad they were saved.

Whenever there is a time of blessing, you can be sure that Satan will stir up trouble, and seek to spoil the work of the Lord if he can. But the apostles were glad to suffer for Christ, and especially since so many had been truly saved. Why should we care about a few insults from some who do not believe, if only some get to know the Lord through our witnessing?

5. At Iconium and Lystra, Paul Is First Worshipped Then Stoned (14:1-18)

From Antioch in Pisidia the apostles go on to Iconium, where they stayed quite a long time, preaching the gospel and healing the sick. The results were much the same; many believed, but the Jews turned on them and stirred up the people to try and stone Paul and Barnabas to death. However, they found out in time and escaped to Lystra, the next big city.

At Lystra Paul healed a lifelong cripple, which made such an impression on the people that they thought Paul and Barnabas must be two of the heathen gods come down in the form of men. They were so sure that they brought animals to offer as a sacrifice to them. This, of course, they refused to accept, for the same reason that Peter told Cornelius to stand up when he had fallen down before him. It is very sinful for any man to accept divine worship. Why is it, when God is so good to us, that men are willing so often to worship any creature, but not God Himself?

6. They Leave Lystra and Return Home to Antioch (14:19-28)

But the mob in Lystra soon changed around, and when the Jews stirred them up against Paul, they became so angry they tried to kill him with stones. When they thought he was dead they left him, but God raised him up again, as He still had a large work for him to do.

Despite this terrible experience, Paul only wants to go on serving the Lord. They went on to Derbe, but then set out on the return journey back to the assembly at Antioch. And far from avoiding those cities where he had been so badly treated, Paul goes right back through them all again, seeking to confirm the souls of those who had been saved when they were there before. He also wanted to see little churches established in every place, so that the Christians could meet together and help each other. Finally they get back to their home church to tell about the wonderful things God had done in saving so many souls.

The Jerusalem Council

1. Dispute with Jewish Christians (15:1-5)

We noted in chapter 11 that some of the Jewish leaders who had believed (or at least said they had) disputed with Peter because he associated with Gentiles. When he explained how the Lord had led, these men could say nothing more.

But here we find them stirring up trouble again and actually travelling to Antioch to tell the Gentile Christians they had to be circumcised. This was the sign in the Old Testament times that a man believed in God and wanted His blessing. It was a good thing at that time, and God had commanded Abraham and others to do so.

But all the Old Testament ceremonies have been fulfilled and done away with in Christ. Moreover, *anything* added to the work of Christ as being necessary for salvation is altogether wrong. Faith in the Lord Jesus and His finished work is the *only* thing necessary for me to be saved. The poor sinner realizes his guilt and has no claim on God except His love. But he does not need any good works of his own, such as circumcision or baptism or church membership. All he needs is Christ and by faith he can make Christ his own. Are you trusting in the blood of Christ or this plus your own works?

The saints at Antioch were perplexed at this wrong teaching, but Paul and Barnabas assured them that it was not true. Still it was decided that they should go to Jerusalem to consult with the church leaders there. The apostles received Paul and Barnabas very nicely but some of the Pharisees who believed insisted that all must be circumcised.

2. Peter Tells How the Spirit Was Given to Gentile Believers (15:6-11)

So they decided to meet together and thoroughly discuss the matter. Most problems and disputes can be settled if people come together and talk things over.

At first there was a great deal of argument, but Peter simply reminded them of how God had in fact received the Gentiles on the basis of their faith. This could be proved because He had given the Holy Spirit to Cornelius and many others. Why then did these former Pharisees seek to put a burden of law-keeping on those whom God had accepted without any such conditions whatever? The Jews themselves could not be saved by keeping the law, only by faith. So why would the Gentiles be forced to do what the Jews had failed to do?

3. Paul, Barnabas and James Speak (15:12-21)

Then Paul and Barnabas tell how God had done wonderful miracles among the Gentiles, for example, the cripple at Lystra had been cured. More wonderful still, hundreds had been saved by believing in Jesus Christ.

Finally James brings in a prophecy from Amos to support Peter's statement that God had accepted Gentiles who called upon His name. This settles the argument and again shows us how important it is to know the whole Word of God, both Old Testament and New Testament.

James' conclusion is that the Gentiles should not be asked to accept circumcision or keep the law of Moses. But the apostles should write to them and tell them to avoid the sins of fornication and idolatry, and certain kinds of food.

This is very good news for all Gentiles as keeping the whole law is a burden. Even the four things prohibited are not said to be the *way* of salvation. Instead they are things which a Christian avoids because he *is* a child of God, not to make himself one.

There is a very important difference here which many Christians do not understand. Good works are the fruit of salvation, not the means. I am saved by the grace of God, but now that I am saved, I *want* to serve Him. And this is not even to keep myself saved, but just to please the Lord, who first loved me.

4. The Letter to Gentile Believers (15:22-29)

James' proposal was well received by all the church and they chose two men, Judas and Silas, to go back to Antioch with the letter. These two are described as "chief men among the brethren" (v. 22). No doubt they deserved this title of honor, but a still better description is found in verse 25. It is better to risk your life to spread the gospel of Christ than to try to become famous even among Christians. Yet some Christians spend their time seeking fame in this world.

In the letter the apostles point out that they had never sent those men in the first place to tell people they had to be circumcised. Instead of this they put no burden upon them except the four necessary things.

5. The Gentiles Receive the Letter with Joy (15:30-35)

When they reach Antioch, they gather the church together and read the letter to them. Many had been really worried about this false doctrine. But now they are greatly relieved to hear that Paul's teaching was correct after all, and one must be saved by faith alone. Furthermore Judas and Silas taught the people and strengthened them in their faith. After a while the brethren let them return to Jerusalem but Silas decided to stay on and help in the work of the Lord.

You might think that this question of keeping the law for salvation had now been settled once and for all. But in Paul's letters we find that the Jews were very active and went to great lengths to impose this doctrine on the people. Paul meets this wrong doctrine in Galatians, 1 Corinthians, Philippians, and Colossians.

6. Paul and Silas Set Out on the Second Missionary Journey (15:36-41)

Soon after Paul proposed to Barnabas that they go again to visit the cities where people had been saved before. Barnabas was willing but insisted on taking his cousin Mark who had dropped out on the first journey. This Paul refused to do and finally they had to go different routes. We do not hear of Barnabas or Mark in Acts, but Paul considered them both friends (1 Corinthians 9:6; 2 Timothy 4:11).

Paul found that Silas was happy to go with him to preach the gospel. The brethren commended them to the grace of God and off they went. It is a good thing to be at all times in God's will.

CHAPTER

8

The Second Round (16:1—18:22)

Memory Verses
Acts 16:30-31; 1 Corinthians 1:18

Main Points of the Lesson

1. Let us obey God's call even if we do not understand.
2. We should not ask for worldly help nor accept it.
3. Being happy in time of trouble will bring a reward.
4. The gospel is a blessing to some people and hardens others.
5. The wise men of this world may be foolish in God's sight.
6. All teaching must be tested by Scripture.

From Antioch to Philippi

1. Paul Chooses Timothy to Go with Them (16:1-5)

When Paul and Barnabas were in Lystra on the first journey, the people first worshipped them then stoned Paul. One young man was deeply impressed with this. He gave his heart to the Lord afresh and longed to help in the work. This was Timothy.

When Paul came back he asked the brethren about Timothy and when he learned how highly they considered him Paul asked if he could go with them. Timothy's father was not Jewish although his mother was. So, to avoid unnecessary criticism from the Jews, Timothy was circumcised. Notice that this was *not* so he would be saved. He was saved by the precious blood of Christ. This was simply to avoid offense to those who felt strongly about the matter. As for Timothy, he was willing to do anything for Christ.

So the three men went on to visit all the churches and tell them the good news that keeping the law is not necessary for conversion. The result was that the churches were established and souls were saved every day.

2. The Macedonian Call (16:6-10)

After going through the countries of Phrygia and Galatia they tried to enter the province of Asia, part of what we call Asia Minor. But the Spirit prevented them from going there and also into Bithynia.

Finally they reached Troas on the northern sea-coast, just across a narrow sea from Macedonia, a country in Europe. At this point Paul saw in a vision a man of Macedonia saying, "Come over into Macedonia and help us." This remarkable experience made all who were with Paul agree that it must be from God, so they made every effort to go. Notice in verse 10 Luke, the author of this book, says, "*We* endeavored, etc." This shows that Luke joined the missionary group at this point.

So the great apostle was called from Asia to Europe to preach the gospel. Soon churches were established and Europe became a stronghold of Christianity for many centuries.

3. At Philippi Lydia Receives the Word (16:11-18)

So when they obeyed, the Lord gave them a good trip and they soon arrived at Philippi, the chief city of that region. Here there was no Jewish synagogue for Paul to preach in but they found a few women by the river side where they used to meet for prayer. One of these in particular was very glad to hear the message and God opened her heart and she believed. She was a seller of purple dye or cloth, and her name was Lydia. She was soon baptized and offered the missionaries a place to live in her home.

Another young woman was in the terrible power of an evil spirit called Python. Because of strange things she said, her masters obtained much gain. But this girl somehow recognized that Paul and Silas were servants of God, and followed them around telling everybody in a loud voice. Of course this was true but Paul would accept no help from one in the grip of Satan. So finally he commanded the evil spirit to come out of her.

4. Paul and Silas Beaten (16:19-24)

Naturally the masters of the girl were angry at Paul and Silas because now they could make no more easy money from her. So they drew them before the magistrates and charged them with causing trouble in the city. The magistrates listened to the mob and did not even ask Paul if these things were true. Instead they simply commanded them to be beaten with a heavy whip. Then they were put in the inner prison, their feet fastened in big wooden stocks so they could not escape.

It was very unrighteous for the magistrates to beat so cruelly men who had done no wrong and were not even allowed to answer for themselves. So Paul and Silas with bleeding backs are spending the night in a cold uncomfortable prison. How did they feel?

5. The Jailer Is Saved (16:25-34)

Paul and Silas had been wrongfully treated but far from feeling bitter about it, or supposing God had forgotten them, they are truly grateful to Him for the privilege of suffering for Christ. So they are heard at midnight singing songs and praying to God. God *always* answers prayer but not always in such a spectacular way. This time He sent an earthquake which shook loose the doors of the prison and also freed every person in it, so they all could have escaped.

When the jailer realized what had happened he knew he would be put to death for letting the prisoners get away (see 12:19). So he pulled out his sword and was just about to kill himself when Paul called out to him to say all were still there. Then the jailer realized God must be in all this and came trembling to ask how to be saved. Naturally Paul and Silas were able to tell him the answer to this and their joy was still greater when he and all his household were saved and baptized that very night. Thus Paul and Silas were faithful in such a time of sorrow and God soon turned their trouble into great joy. We should be prepared to accept all circumstances from God and trust Him to make up for all wrongs.

6. Paul and Silas Are Released and Leave the City (16:35-40)

Even the magistrates next morning felt they had gone too far and quietly told the jailer to let them go. But now Paul refused to go. Actually Paul and Silas were Roman citizens and they could get the magistrates into real trouble for beating them without a fair trial. This Paul did not intend to do, but neither did he want the people of Philippi to think that the gospel was being preached by persons without any rights. So the magistrates themselves came and released them from prison.

After they had seen the brethren again at Lydia's home, they left the city. So the gospel entered Europe. The missionaries had joy at seeing souls saved, more joy when allowed to suffer for Christ, still more when others got saved as a result of their cheerful suffering.

On to Athens and Back to Antioch

1. In Thessalonica: Blessing and Persecution (17:1-9)

The next city they came to was Thessalonica, the capital of Macedonia. Here as usual, Paul went into the synagogue, and preached from the Scriptures that Christ should suffer then be glorified, and that Jesus was the Christ. As usual, some believed and some refused. Then the Jews started trouble, and accused the missionaries of disloyalty to the Emperor. It was true that Paul preached Jesus the King, but he did not teach that people should disobey their ruler.

Paul's experience at Thessalonica must have been very similar to that of many other places. In fact, whenever the gospel is preached in the power of the Holy Spirit, it will result in blessing and opposition. Some receive the gift of eternal life, and others show that in rejecting Christ they are opposed to all that is of God. It is a serious thing to hear the gospel, because so much depends on what you do about it. It is also serious when the gospel is preached, as those who hear are either being drawn to God, or else being hardened.

It is interesting to read Paul's two letters to the church of the Thessalonians after reading in Acts the story of his visit.

2. In Berea: The People Search the Scriptures (17:10-15)

When the missionaries were sent away from one city because of persecution, they simply went on to another. Here in Berea, they found people more willing to hear, and Luke says that these people were more noble than those of Thessalonica. They listened to the message of Paul with an open mind yet did not receive everything he said without thought. On the contrary, they searched the Scriptures to see if these things were really so.

There are so many different doctrines in the world, each claiming to be true, that a Christian must learn to test everything by the Word of God. We can always learn from other people, but if their teaching is denied by the Scriptures, we will not only refuse to accept it, but try to warn others also. Here Paul was a great teacher, but the Bereans tested everything with this: "What saith the Lord?" The Bible is our only source of certainty with regard to God and salvation.

Now of course this is just what Paul wanted, as his preaching was exactly what the Bible said. THEREFORE many of them believed. But the Jews from Thessalonica soon got busy, and Paul had to leave. However, Silas and Timothy stayed for a while, and the church was established.

3. Athens: The People Listen with Interest (17:16-21)

Athens was the big university center of the ancient world. Many great philosophers had lived there, and in Paul's time some of the people were interested in their teachings. It was also a very religious city in that there were hundreds of idols to the many gods which were worshipped by the Athenians. Paul not only preached to the Jews in the synagogue, but, being greatly moved by the idolatry of Athens, he went right out into the market and spoke to all who would listen to him. Now the Athenians were always looking for some new teaching, so when they heard Paul speaking in this way, they took him to a kind of court on the hill, and asked him to explain this new teaching to them.

The men of Athens apparently had an open mind, like those of Berea, but they did not believe the Scripture, nor were they willing to accept Paul's message. One is bound to admire the great philosophers of ancient Greece but the human mind, without revelation from God, is incapable of finding out the truth of God. So today wise men are able to think through many wonderful things, but as their minds are closed to the light of God's revelation, they are unable to come to the truth. To enter the kingdom of heaven we must become as little children.

4. The Athenians Mock Paul's Message (17:22-34)

In this passage we have Paul's famous speech at Athens. He does not quote from Scripture, as these listeners are heathen people, not Jews. He tells them that the Creator God is a God of love, but He will judge the world in justice for its sin in departing from Him. The Judge of all will be the one whom God raised from the dead (the Lord Jesus Christ). But before Paul can finish what he wants to say about Christ, the people began laughing, as they did not believe in the resurrection. Others more politely said they would hear him again. Perhaps they had another opportunity. But those who were polite and those who were rude both rejected the truth about Jesus, hence there was no salvation for them. Some, however, did believe and so Paul's heart was cheered.

5. At Corinth: Paul Teaches for a Year and a Half (18:1-11)

So Paul went on to Corinth, another very large city, mostly filled with heathen people. Here he met Aquila and Priscilla, a Jewish couple who made their living by making tents. Paul had learned how to make tents when a boy, and as it was his custom to work for a living as well as preach the gospel, he worked with these two.

When Silas and Timothy came from Berea, they preached together and many Jews believed, but some were violently opposed to the truth. So Paul told them that he would turn to the Gentiles and tell them the way of salvation. Then the Lord gave Paul a special vision of encouragement, and so they stayed on there for one and a half years. The Lord never allows us too much discouragement. Here He especially wanted Paul to preach to the Gentiles, and His obedient servant stayed on fulfilling His Lord's command.

6. Paul Returns to Antioch (18:12-22)

Finally the Jews caught Paul and brought a charge against him to Gallio, the ruler, hoping that they could punish or kill him. But Gallio refused to hear this case, because it had to do purely with their religion. So they turned their spite against Sosthenes the ruler of the synagogue and beat him right before Gallio, but it made no difference to him.

So Paul left Corinth with Priscilla and Aquila. They went to Ephesus and Paul went to Caesarea and Jerusalem, then back to Antioch, where he had first started from (15:35, 40). What a grand story he must have told them of all the way God had led and blessed!

CHAPTER

9

More Worlds to Conquer (18:23—20:38)

Memory Verses
John 14:12; 2 Timothy 4:7-8

Main Points of the Lesson

1. Acting like Christ proves that I have the Holy Spirit.
2. Satan tries to imitate the works of God.
3. Christians do not need good-luck charms.
4. We must show God's love in order to win others.
5. Giving brings more joy than receiving.
6. A life of faithful service to the Lord will have a great reward.

Revival at Ephesus

1. The Travels of Paul and Apollos (18:23-28)

While Paul was visiting again the assemblies of Galatia and Phrygia, two countries in what we now call Asia Minor, Apollos came to Ephesus. Apollos was an African Jew, born in Alexandria. He was a good speaker, and knew the Old Testament very well indeed. Also he was very earnest in teaching the things of the Lord. He knew John the Baptist had said Christ was soon coming, but he did not know much else about the Lord Jesus.

There were two people who heard him preach in the synagogue who really knew more about Christianity than he did: Aquila and Priscilla. So they took him and told him more about the ways of God as seen in the Lord Jesus Christ. Aquila was no great preacher but only a tent-maker (18:3). It is good that Apollos was not too proud to learn from these fine people, even though he was already a great preacher. With this new and more wonderful knowledge, Apollos wanted to go into Greece and there preach Christ, the only Savior.

2. Paul at Ephesus: The Disciples of John (19:1-7)

While Apollos was in Corinth, a large city of Greece, Paul reached Ephesus. There he found twelve men, who had been baptized but like Apollos knew little about Christ. So Paul taught them more about the Lord Jesus, and they were baptized in His name. After this, the Holy Spirit came upon them in power, and they began to speak in tongues just like the disciples in Jerusalem had done on the day of Pentecost.

Today people are baptized after they are saved, but we receive the Holy Spirit when we are born again. And the sign that we have the Holy Spirit is that we show forth the glories of the Lord Jesus. The Holy Spirit will help us to be kind and truthful and become more Christ like. It is hard for people to believe that we really have the Spirit of Christ if we do not act as He did.

3. Paul Preaches and Does Many Miracles (19:8-16)

After this Paul preached for three months in the synagogue, but when the Jews absolutely refused his message of Christ, he moved out and began to preach in the school of Tyrannus. This continued for two years, and the gospel message spread all over the province of Asia.

In order to prove to all the people that the preaching of Paul was really true, God gave him special power to perform miracles at Ephesus, greater than anything he had done before. The Lord Jesus had said that when the Holy Spirit was come, His disciples would do greater things than even He had done (John 14:12). Even pieces of cloth from Paul were sufficient to heal many that were sick or afflicted with evil spirits.

Whenever God begins a great work, we can be sure that Satan will try to spoil it. If he cannot stop it, he sometimes tries to imitate it so that ordinary people will hardly be able to tell what is of God and what of Satan. So here we find seven men trying to drive out an evil spirit in the name of Jesus and Paul. But this did not work at all, and in fact, they were wounded and put to shame. Even in our prayers, it is not merely saying the name of Jesus that counts, but true faith in the promises of God.

4. Many Believe at Ephesus (19:17-22)

When the false work of Satan was exposed and everybody knew it, the name of the Lord Jesus was magnified still more. The result was that many who practiced witchcraft brought their books and burned them publicly. These books of secrets had cost a great deal of money and could have been sold to others. But these men proved that they really believed in God by the fact that they no longer wanted to make money by evil practices. It is no use saying you are a Christian, if you act in many ways just like other people who are not saved at all.

But despite all this great blessing, Paul kept thinking about the other Christians in Macedonia and Greece and Rome. He made up his mind to go and visit them, but first sent Timothy and Erastus.

5. Demetrius and the Silversmiths (19:23-28)

Satan had failed in trying to imitate the power of God, so now he stirs up trouble for the saints in another way. Demetrius and the other silversmiths made a lot of money out of the false religion of Diana. They made little silver images and sold them at a high price to the people, who thought that these would bring them good luck. When the people learned the love of God as revealed in Christ Jesus, they no longer wanted these things which reminded them of their old Satanic religion. When the silversmiths found business getting bad, they blamed Paul, and tried to start a riot against him.

Many people make lots of money through false religions. They are the ones who especially try to keep people from believing the truth. They think more about their money than about the souls of men.

6. The Whole City in an Uproar (19:29-41)

The people caught some of Paul's companions, but his friends kept him from rushing into the place of danger. The mob kept crying out for about two hours: "Great is Diana of the Ephesians." Finally the town clerk was able to silence the people and they stopped shouting and went home more quietly. So once again the danger passed and the apostle escaped harm and danger. It is good to know that God always has means of delivering His servants even when things look the blackest. Fear should never keep us from doing great things for God.

Towards Jerusalem

1. From Ephesus to Greece and Back to Troy (20:1-6)

When the trouble at Ephesus was over, Paul went into Macedonia and then into Greece, probably Corinth. But after three months the Jews again made a plot to kill him, and so he left and headed back for Asia Minor and Syria.

It is very interesting to know something about the places which Paul visited and the people who travelled with him. Everywhere he went he preached Christ to men and women with never-dying souls. Some of these became Christians and some of them wanted to help Paul in the work of the Lord. In verse 4 we have the names of seven men who had the privilege of travelling and living with Paul for a while. Paul was a great man, able to reach others and draw them to Christ. All Christians should show forth the love of God and be kind to other people in order to win them for the Lord.

2. Paul Raises a Young Man (20:7-12)

Finally Paul got to Troas again and stayed there, one week. On Sunday, the first day of the week, the disciples came together in an upper room to remember the Lord in the breaking of bread. Paul preached to them at great length, in fact all night long. He must have been a wonderful speaker, and of course the people were very much interested in what he had to say.

But about midnight one young man who was sitting in a window, dropped asleep and fell out of the window from the third story to the ground, and was taken up dead. But Paul went down and comforted the people by assuring them that he was alive again. So Paul was able to continue his message until the morning.

3. Paul Travels On by Foot (20:13-16)

There were seven men travelling with Paul whose names are given, but we know that Luke, the writer of this book, was with him also because he uses the word "we." What a grand group of men and what fellowship they must have had in the work of the Lord! It is clear from 24:17 that Paul with the others was bringing a gift of money to poor saints at Jerusalem. Perhaps this is one reason why he wanted so many to travel with him. The money had been given by the various churches, and these men would be witnesses that Paul had really taken it all to those for whom it was intended. Another thing, it was very dangerous travelling in those days when there were no policemen. If some one tried to rob Paul of this large sum of money, it would be better to have some friends near to help.

Paul decided to walk the twenty miles over land and join the others when the ship reached the other side. Walking is a very valuable form of exercise, and some exercise is necessary for good health. Paul knew that his body was the temple of the Holy Spirit, and wanted to keep fit and well so that he could serve the Lord as much as possible.

4. Paul's Farewell Address to the Ephesian Elders (20:17-27)

Paul did not want to go to Ephesus at this time, as he knew it would be hard to get away again. The people would want him to stay and teach them the Word of God. So he sent word and some of the older men who were in charge of the church came down to the port of Miletus. There Paul had a long talk with them, reminding them of his work among them, and warning them of trouble ahead.

Without boasting in any way, Paul shows us here how he had served the Lord in Ephesus for three years, working for his own living, preaching to them publicly and visiting in their homes to tell them more about Christ. He preached to them "repentance toward God and faith toward our Lord Jesus Christ" (v. 21). He testified "the gospel of the grace of God" and preached the "Kingdom of God" among them (vv. 24-25) at all seasons (v. 18) night and day (v. 31). Indeed, he did not shun to declare unto them the whole counsel of God (v. 27) and that despite all his difficulties from the Jews (v. 19).

What a wonderful example of faithful and loyal service to the One whom he loved and was determined to serve to the very end! Each of us should in our own way try to serve the Lord faithfully.

5. Paul Warns Them of Dangers Ahead (20:28-35)

There was a fine strong church at Ephesus and Paul had done a great deal to establish them in the truth of God. Yet he knew that sinful men would come in from outside and seek to destroy the work of the Lord. Worse still, from among the members of the church, there would come men who would teach things not true to God's word.

Paul had had experience of the evil some of these false teachers could do in other places. So here he warns them to be on their guard against these wicked men, to take care of themselves and the rest of the church. We see in Revelation 2:4 that the church at Ephesus did leave its first love, so we know that Satan is always busy trying to spoil the work of the Lord.

6. Love and Sorrow (20:36-38)

After warning these men of evil days to come, Paul knelt down and prayed with them, commending them to God and to the word of His grace (v. 32). They all wept and kissed him, but most of all they were sorry for his word that some of them would see him again no more. Actually it was about eight years later before he got back there, but he had the consolation that the Holy Spirit would care for all the people of God. The elders could rejoice in this too as they started the 28-mile journey back again to Ephesus.

CHAPTER

10

Paul Is Arrested (21—24)

Memory Verses
Acts 22:15; 24:25

Main Points of the Lesson

1. We should try to please people so as to win them for Christ.
2. The majority of people may be wrong.
3. God is faithful in looking after His children.
4. God is able to protect His servants at all times.
5. Many will be lost because they delayed too long.
6. It is wrong to confess something you did not do.

Paul in Jerusalem

1. The Spirit Warns Paul Not to Go to Jerusalem (21:1-14)

From Ephesus Paul and his company continued on their way to Jerusalem. They stopped for a short time at Tyre and Caesarea, and of course, wanted to visit the Christians in those places. In Tyre, the disciples told him through the Spirit that he should not go up to Jerusalem. In Caesarea a prophet called Agabus told him that he would be bound and turned over to the Gentile rulers in Jerusalem.

Paul was anxious to deliver personally the money for the poor in Jerusalem. He also wanted to preach the pure gospel and teach the Christians in that city. Many there were not very clear on how to be saved, thinking that it was necessary to obey the law for salvation. We see in these verses that he was not afraid of the Jews or the Gentiles and was ready to go to prison or die for the sake of the Lord Jesus. Why are *we* ever afraid to witness for the Lord?

2. The Brethren Receive Them with Joy (21:15-26)

When they reached Jerusalem, the brethren were very happy to see them, and to hear the good news of God's blessing among the Gentiles. No doubt they were glad also to receive the gift of money which the missionaries had brought.

There were thousands of believing Jews, however, in the city who were suspicious of Paul, because they thought that he no longer cared about the Old Testament laws. The elder brethren therefore suggested that he should go through a certain ceremony which would please these Jews and make Paul more popular with them. Sometimes it is wise to do little things to please others, as long as there is nothing wrong in it which would spoil our testimony. Paul really wishes to give them the gospel in all its purity, but going through this ceremony did not give him the opportunity which he wanted.

3. Paul Arrested (21:27-40)

Just when the seven days were almost up, some of the unbelieving Jews saw Paul in the temple, and started a riot against him. This was their opportunity to kill him, and they lost no time. But when the chief captain, Claudius Lysias, heard the uproar he immediately sent some soldiers to keep the mob in order. They seized Paul and bound him with two chains and took him to the castle.

Even there, the people cried out that Paul should be killed. But Paul asked permission to speak to the chief captain, who was surprised that Paul knew the Greek language. Then Paul told him he was a Jew of Tarsus, an important city, and so he was given permission to speak to the people in his own defense.

We have often seen in this book how a crowd or mob tried to attack or kill the servant of the Lord. It is well to note that the majority is not always right, and the Lord's blessing is on the one who stands for the truth, even though every one is against him.

4. *Paul's Defense: He Received the Light (22:1-10)*

Paul in explaining why he was a Christian went right back to the beginning. He said that he was educated right there in Jerusalem by a famous teacher, Gamaliel. He had been so zealous in the Jewish religion that he had persecuted the Christians and put them in prison.

Next he told how on the way to Damascus he had seen the bright light from heaven, and heard the Voice asking why he was persecuting Him. Then the Lord commanded him to go into Damascus, and he would be told what to do next.

We have read this story before in chapter 9, but Paul loved to tell how he got saved. And no wonder! The Psalmist said, "Let the redeemed of the Lord say so." Does everyone in your family and neighborhood know that you belong to Christ? Have you confessed Him at school or work and amongst your friends? Some day we will be proud that we belong to Jesus; we should not be ashamed now.

5. *Paul Tells of His Vision at Jerusalem (22:11-21)*

Paul goes on to tell that when he entered Damascus, he was visited by Ananias, a devout man, who told him that the God of their fathers had chosen him to be a witness to all men. So he had been baptized.

Then when he had come again to Jerusalem, actually in the temple, the Lord had appeared to him in a trance, and told him to leave the city, because the people would not receive his testimony. Instead he was to go far away and preach to the Gentiles. So the good news of salvation which the Jews were still refusing was to be given to the Gentiles, and Paul could state that many thousands of them had believed. So we see that the plans of God cannot fail. If some refuse the blessing He wishes to give, there are others who will accept. Let us be sure that we do not refuse God's best for us.

6. *The Chief Captain Saves Paul from the Jews (22:22-30)*

At this point, the Jews refused to listen any longer. To think that the Gentiles might get their blessing was too much. So they cried out again that he should be killed. The chief captain could not understand their hatred, so thought that if Paul was beaten he would tell the real reason. But when Paul told him that he was a Roman citizen, he decided not to do this, as it was against the law. So he had to give Paul protection, and kept him under guard that night. Thus we see that the Lord was still looking after His faithful servant, and He is just the same today.

Paul Goes to Caesarea

1. Before the Council at Jerusalem (23:1-11)

The next morning Paul was brought by the chief captain to stand before the high priest and all the council. When Paul stated that he had always had a good conscience before God, the high priest was so annoyed that he commanded some soldiers standing near to slap his mouth. This was so unfair that Paul in turn became angry, and called him a whited wall. But as soon as he knew that it was the high priest he apologized, as the Bible says we should not say evil things about the ruler of the people.

No doubt it was hard for Paul to stand quietly while some one slapped him, but we are reminded of how gracious and patient the Lord Jesus was when standing in the same place. A Roman soldier slapped Him, but He did not return evil for evil. (See John 18:23.)

There was then more quarrelling in the court, and finally the chief captain again had to rescue Paul and put him in the castle. But that night the Lord appeared to Paul and promised him that he would be able to witness for Him at Rome.

2. Forty Men Swear That They Will Kill Paul (23:12-24)

When the Jews saw that they again had failed to accomplish Paul's death some of them made a plot and swore that they would not eat or drink until they had murdered him. The plan was to ask the chief captain to send him again to the high priest, and they would kill him on the way. But fortunately for Paul, his nephew heard about the plot and came and told him. When the chief captain knew about it, he ordered 470 men to protect Paul and take him to the governor at Caesarea.

Once again we see Satan's different means of attacking the servants of God. Note that these men, who thought they were being very religious, could actually prepare to commit murder. We also see that God has His own people ready to protect and help His faithful witnesses. We can be sure that nothing can happen to the child of God without the Father knowing about it, and first providing some way of escape. We do not even know the name of Paul's nephew, but he saw his duty and did it faithfully. The result was that Paul was able to serve the Lord for perhaps nine years more.

3. *The Chief Captain Sends Paul to Caesarea (23:25-35)*

Felix was the governor appointed by Rome to rule Judea. The chief captain thought it would be safer to get Paul away from Jerusalem and into the care of Felix himself. So he wrote a letter explaining that Paul was a Roman citizen and that he had done nothing worthy of death or bonds. Then he told about the plot of the Jews to kill Paul, which was his reason for sending him to the governor. The foot-soldiers went half way with them, then returned. But those on horse-back took Paul right to the governor at Caesarea. Felix when he read the letter, asked Paul where he came from, and then commanded that he should be kept until the time of his trial.

The Romans were noted for their high regard for law and order. Yet many individual rulers were corrupt and unrighteous. We know that Pilate, a Roman governor, had given in to the Jews when they demanded the death of the Lord. And in Acts many who were supposed to guard the Roman law, did not hesitate to do wrong if they could make a little money by it.

4. *Tertullus Accuses Paul Before Felix (24:1-9)*

Five days later, the high priest came from Jerusalem with many others to press their charges against Paul. With them was a professional orator named Tertullus, who when the trial came, made a speech against Paul before Felix.

At first he sought to flatter the governor, then stated that Paul was a ringleader of the Nazarenes, and had tried to bring Gentiles into the holy temple. The Jews who were with him agreed that everything he said was true. In a sense part of it was true, but he tried to make it look as bad as possible so that they would get Paul into trouble with the governor. It is possible to say something more or less true, but in such a way as to give a wrong impression. "God desireth truth in the inward parts."

5. *Paul's Reply Before Felix (24:10-21)*

Paul in his reply first denied that he had stirred up any trouble in Jerusalem. It was even then only 12 days since he had come to Jerusalem with an offering for the people, and they had not found him speaking to the crowd either in the temple or the city. However, he did admit that he was a heretic according to their way of thinking, in that he was a follower of Jesus. But he believed in the Old Testament, the resurrection, and worshipped the God of their fathers. So here Paul is ready to admit any possible wrong which he had done, but will not falsely confess to any crime. He also (as ever) is glad to confess to his faith in the Lord Jesus, and if that means death for him, still he is ready.

6. Felix Is Afraid, But Leaves Paul in Prison (24:22-27)

So Felix decided that they would have to wait until the chief captain came down from Jerusalem. He gave Paul a good deal of liberty, including visits from his friends. We know that Luke was with him, and Philip lived in Caesarea, and no doubt others came also.

When Felix' wife came, Paul had an opportunity to give them both the gospel, and Felix as he listened was really impressed. But instead of accepting the Lord then and there, he put it off until another day. There will be very many millions lost forever because they put off God's offer of salvation. Felix was more interested in money, and hoped that Paul would bribe him to get out of prison. He also wanted to please the Jews so he left Paul in prison for two years.

CHAPTER

11

The Appeal to Caesar (25—26)

Memory Verse
Acts 26:19

Main Points of the Lesson

1. When Christ comes He will set all things right.
2. The gospel leaves no room for religious pride.
3. To be "almost saved" is to be lost.

Paul Answers Before Festus and Appeals to Caesar (25:1-12)

Felix was such a bad governor that finally he was forced out by the Roman government. When Festus came to take his place, he found Paul still in the prison. He was another one who tried to please the Jews. But when they again made a plot to kill Paul if Festus would send him to Jerusalem, he refused to do so. Rather he told them to come to Caesarea and lay their charges against him in court.

This they did, accusing Paul of many things, all untrue. At last Festus asked Paul if he would agree to go to Jerusalem again for a trial, but Paul refused. As a Roman citizen he had the right to ask that his case be heard in Rome itself by Caesar. When Paul saw that he would never get a fair trial there in the land of the Jews, he felt compelled to appeal to Caesar.

Often in this world men fail to obtain justice, and unrighteousness seems to reign. But some day God, the righteous Judge, will set all things right. (See 2 Thessalonians 1:6.)

Festus Tells King Agrippa About Paul (25:13-22)

A little later, King Agrippa came along with Bernice, to visit Caesarea, and to greet Festus the new governor. Festus told Agrippa about Paul, how the Jews had accused him so bitterly, and how he had appealed to Caesar. King Agrippa had heard a good deal about Paul and was rather curious to know more about him. So they agreed to call him and hear his story the next day.

This man Agrippa had another name, Herod. He was the son of King Herod who killed James with the sword (Acts 12:1-2). His great grandfather had tried to kill the Lord Jesus (Matthew 2:13). His father's uncle, also called Herod, had mocked the Lord Jesus at the time of His death (Luke 23:11). So Paul probably realized that he could not expect much righteous judgment from such a man. It seems strange that these wicked men should sit in judgment on a true servant of the most High God. For the present God has left the control of things in the hands of sinful men. But soon He will take charge and all unfairness and sin will be revealed and judged.

The Beginning of the Trial (25:23-27)

This is really the fifth time that Paul has appeared before the people and spoken in his own defense. More than two years have gone by since he was first nearly killed by the mob of fanatics in Jerusalem.

When the time came, King Agrippa came in with Bernice with great pomp and show, together with the important men of the city. Finally Paul was brought in and introduced by Festus, who thought it was unreasonable to send a prisoner to Caesar without stating exactly what the charges were against him.

What a contrast between Paul and his judge! We have seen what a wicked man Agrippa was. He was living in sin with Bernice who was not really his wife. Festus was a better type of person, but he was a man-pleaser and although he should have released Paul before, he had refused to do so. Yet Paul, as we shall see, when he had the opportunity to speak for himself, did so courteously and, as always, witnessed for the Lord Jesus.

Paul's Defense: His Former Religion (26:1-11)

What seemed odd to Paul was that he had always been a good Jew, and in early days had been more zealous than others. The most important point of the Jewish religion was that they looked forward to the coming of the Messiah or King, also called Christ. Now He had come, Paul believed on Him, and for this the Jews were persecuting him to the death!

Religion is always opposed to Christ. All religions of the world say, "Do this, or that, and you will be saved." In this way there is something for man to boast about. But Christ says, "I paid the price of your salvation, I did it all, and finished the work." There is thus no room for human pride and so religious men hate the gospel of Christ.

Paul's Defense: He Found Christ (26:12-23)

This is the third time in Acts we have read the story of Paul's conversion. All Scripture is given by inspiration of God and is profitable. Nothing is added unnecessarily and nothing of value for us is left out. So when we find three times in this one book the account of how Paul was saved, we can see how important it was. The greatest persecutor of Christians became one himself at that moment. More than that he became perhaps the greatest servant of Christ ever to live.

For Paul himself, he never tired of telling how God in mercy saved his soul. Here he says, "I was not disobedient to the heavenly vision." If God has enabled you to see Jesus Christ dying on the cross for your sins, do not disobey the vision by refusing Him as your Savior. If he has given you a vision of serving Him, perhaps in some distant land, be sure you do not fail.

They Command That Paul Be Sent to Rome (26:24-32)

As he spoke, Festus thought he was going out of his mind. King Agrippa said, "Almost thou persuadest me to be a Christian." Neither of them believed Paul's message. Neither of them was saved. Some reject the gospel with scorn, even calling Christians insane. Others are almost ready to accept the truth. "Almost cannot avail, Almost is but to fail; Sad, sad that bitter wail: Almost, but lost." Let the student be sure just now that he is really saved. If not, put your trust in Christ right where you are. He will accept you and save and keep you forever.

CHAPTER

12

Perils and Prison (27—28)

Memory Verses
Acts 27:25; 28:24

Main Points of the Lesson

1. Instead of making our own plans we should seek God's will.
2. The man in touch with God is the best leader to follow.
3. God may allow us to go through trials, but He will never forsake us.
4. Most people will respond gratefully to kindness.
5. When the gospel is preached some believe and some refuse.
6. The story of Acts continues to this day.

The Journey to Rome

1. Paul and Luke, with Julius: They Reach Crete (27:1-8)

Once it was decided that Paul should indeed go to Rome to be heard by Caesar, no time was lost in turning him over to a captain named Julius, who became responsible to take him all the way. Luke, the beloved physician, and another Christian named Aristarchus, went along also.

The small sailing vessels used in those days were not very safe, and the sailors had to keep close to the coastline as much as possible. First the ship stopped at Sidon, and the captain kindly let Paul go ashore and meet some of the friends there. Then they passed by Cyprus, a large island where Paul and Barnabas had preached on the first missionary journey. They put into shore again and changed ships, this time reaching the island of Crete.

After the rough treatment Paul received from the Jews, it is good to see a Roman officer treating him with kindness. So God looks after His people, never leaving His love for them. But still there was plenty of trouble just ahead, as we shall see.

2. A Great Storm (27:9-20)

Paul had had a good deal of experience for the past twenty years in travelling around, sometimes by sea and sometimes by land. Perhaps the Lord especially revealed to him that there was danger ahead. So he warned them that they had better stay in the port of Fair Havens for the winter as the Mediterranean Sea can be very rough at that time of year. But the Roman captain believed the master and owner of the ship, and they decided to go to another port, only twenty miles away, which would be a better place to spend the winter.

At first the wind blew gently, and they made good progress. But soon a stormy wind came up which took them miles off their course. They could no longer control the ship, and they began to throw the cargo overboard, then even the tackle and equipment. It was so cloudy that they saw neither sun nor stars for many days, and so were not able to tell where they were. Finally, they gave up all hope of ever reaching land again.

Many plans are formed contrary to God's mind, and at first circumstances seem to favor them. But soon the wind changes and shipwreck seems certain. These men probably thought that they should have listened to Paul's advice in the beginning.

3. Paul Cheers the People (27:21-26)

Just as Paul had been able to warn them not to start off on this journey, so now he can assure them that in spite of this error and all the trouble they had seen, all would be saved. God told him that he must stand before Caesar, and He would spare the lives of all men aboard for Paul's sake. Paul believed God and exhorted the others to take courage, and believe His promise also.

Here we see Paul the prisoner really the man who knew more about God's will and what would take place than those who kept him as a prisoner. So it is always. The man in touch with God who is desirous of doing His will, neither fearing man nor seeking his favor—this one is really superior to those who seem to be in charge of the situation.

4. The Sailors Wish to Forsake the Ship (27:27-32)

Paul had said that they would be cast on a certain island, and on the fourteenth night, the sailors thought they were drawing near the shore. Now the only lifeboat was too small for all the soldiers and sailors, so some of these tried to get off by themselves, and leave the others to their doom.

Here again Paul was aware of their deceitful trick, and so warned the Roman captain that it should be prevented. So the soldiers cut the ropes of the lifeboat and let it fall into the sea. So we see the prisoner, but the man of God, really in charge of the situation. "Those who honor me will I honor." Some people always are ready to leave or try to escape when things are not going well. And it does not matter to them what happens to anybody else. They think only of their own selfish interests.

5. Paul Asks the Men to Take Some Food (27:33-37)

The storm had been so fierce, and the men so afraid, that they had not even stopped to eat food for two whole weeks. They were still in very grave danger, but Paul had told them that they would all be saved. So they had better eat some food and regain a little strength so as better to be able to save themselves when they did sight land.

So Paul set a good example, took some bread, gave thanks before them all, and began to eat. When they saw his example, the rest also were encouraged and began to eat, 276 people in all. In times of trouble men who know not God tend to get excited and lose their heads. But if you trust in the Lord, you can not only keep calm yourself, but also be a great help to others.

6. All Are Saved (27:38-44)

Sure enough when it was day, they could see the land. But the wind was still strong, and blowing straight for the shore. So they hoisted a sail, and made for the land, hoping to reach a small inlet. But the ship ran ashore, and stuck fast, until the force of the waves broke the stern and it was in danger of sinking. Now the soldiers were responsible for the prisoners, and if they escaped, the soldiers would be killed (12:19 and 16:27). So they wanted to kill the prisoners, but the captain wanted to save Paul, so kept them from doing it. So finally all got to land, all were saved, just as Paul had said by the word of the Lord. God always keeps His promises and looks after His own.

Paul Arrives at Rome

1. The People of Malta Help the Shipwrecked Travellers (28:1-6)

When they got ashore it was still raining, and very cold. The people of the island told them it was called Melita (or Malta) and helped them get warm around a huge fire. We have seen that through this time of trouble, Paul, the man who belonged to God, was the true leader of the group. Now, although nearly sixty years old, and as much exhausted as any of them, he went off and brought a bundle of wood for the fire. As he was laying this on the fire, a snake seized his hand and bit him. But Paul knew the protecting hand of the Lord and instead of becoming panicky, he merely shook off the snake into the fire.

The natives of the island, however, at first thought that as he was a prisoner, he perhaps was a murderer, and although he had not drowned, yet vengeance would see that he did not escape death. But when nothing happened to Paul, they changed their minds and decided that instead he must be a god. But those who know the Lord are not surprised that He kept His servant from the dangers of the sea as well as poisonous snakes.

2. Paul Heals the Sick People of the Island (28:7-10)

The chief man of the island, named Publius, also was very kind to Paul and Luke, and kept them in his own house for three days, probably until some more permanent arrangements could be made. Now God is debtor to no man, and so He enabled His servant first to heal the father of Publius who was sick with a fever. Then the people of the island, who had also showed them a great deal of kindness, brought those who were sick, and the Lord healed them. So to show their gratitude, the people brought gifts to help Paul and Luke on their way.

Even heathen people respond to kindness. The Lord when here on earth went everywhere doing good. Our job as Christians is to "make the love of God credible" by showing kindness to all whom we meet. If we do, people will respond by listening courteously at least to our message about the love of God.

3. The Brethren at Rome Receive Paul and Luke (28:11-16)

After three months, they boarded ship again to complete their journey. At one place where they stopped they found some Christians and stayed there for seven days. Then when they got near Rome, the brethren came to meet them, and this was a great cheer to Paul. He had longed to see them for many years; (see Romans 1:10-13) which was written three years before. Paul had been a prisoner for over two years, and had experienced dreadful things on his way to Rome. Now what a joy to meet the saints there at last!

Finally at Rome, the captain delivered all the prisoners to the man in charge, but Paul was allowed to live by himself, with one soldier to look after him. The captain at least knew that this prisoner was different from the ordinary, and that God was with him. The prisons in those days were very unhealthy places, and it was a good thing that Paul had so much liberty.

4. Paul Calls the Elders of the Jews (28:17-22)

After only three days, Paul at once called the chief of the Jews together to tell them why he had appealed to Caesar. It was not to lay any charge against his own people, but purely in self-defense. He recounts to them the main facts about why he had come to Rome.

The Jews at Rome had received no letters from Jerusalem as to why they were accusing Paul so bitterly, so they could not lay a charge against him before Caesar. They were desirous, however, of learning more about Paul's doctrine, because they had heard so much against it.

Paul said that he was bound with a chain for the hope of Israel. From Old Testament days, faithful Jews had been waiting and hoping for the One whom the prophets had promised, the Messiah, the King of Israel. Finally He had come, Jesus of Nazareth, and God had shown His approval of His Son. The Jewish nation had rejected the very One they had been waiting for, and now Paul is a prisoner because he believed in Christ. This is a great example of how Satan can blind the eyes of men, even religious men.

5. Some Accept the Gospel, Some Reject It (28:23-29)

Paul was glad that the Jews at Rome were open-minded as it gave him another chance to preach the gospel. They set a day, and came to Paul's house, as of course, Paul could not go to the synagogue. From morning to night Paul simply took the Old Testament and showed them that the prophecies of the Messiah had been fulfilled in Christ. The result was the same as always, some believed the things which were spoken and some believed not.

Finally Paul quoted from the book of Isaiah a passage which told about the refusal of the Jews to believe the message of God. Because of their rejection of the gospel, Paul says that he would have to turn to the Gentiles, as he had done so often before in other cities. So the Jews went off and had a great discussion themselves. But those who reject the light will get greater darkness.

6. Paul Lives Two Years in His Own Rented House (28:30, 31)

The Book of Acts is the beginning of the Church, and tells how the gospel went out to all the world. We have read about Paul, but Luke does not tell us the end of the story or what happened next. Actually, the history goes right on, even to the present day. The Lord's disciples are still obeying His command to witness to Him, unto the uttermost parts of the earth. The Acts of the Holy Spirit continue to this day. You can have a part in this great work. Christ expects you to do your share.